CANADA'S FIGHTING PILOTS

NATIONAL LIBRARY OF CANADA CATALOGUING IN PUBLICATION

Cosgrove, Edmund, 1926
      Canada's Fighting Pilots/Edmund Cosgrove.—Rev. ed.

Includes bibliographical references.
ISBN 0-919614-97-3

1. World War, 1939-1945—Aerial operations, Canadian.
2. World War, 1914-1918—Aerial operations, Canadian.
3. Air pilots, Military—Canada—History.
I. Title.

UG635.C2C62003   940.54'4971'0922   C2003-900767-7

Cover design and layout by gordongroup, Ottawa, Canada.

Printed in Canada.

. Published by:
      The Golden Dog Press, an imprint of Haymax Inc.
      P.O. Box 393—Kemptville, Ontario, Canada K0G 1J0

The Golden Dog Press wishes to express its gratitude to the Canada Council, the Ontario Arts Council and the Millennium Bureau of Canada for past support extended to its publishing projects.

Edmund Cosgrove

Canada's FIGHTING PILOTS

With an introduction by Brick Billing

The Golden Dog Press

Ottawa—2003

Acknowledgements

The publishers and the editor would like to thank the following people for their help in the preparation of this book; Chris Carruthers of TextAlchemy, Inc. for his assistance in OCR scanning; John Lund of the London Free Press and DND for their help in obtaining photographs (and with cutline information). Every effort has been made to trace ownership and copyright. The publishers would welcome any information that would help with these acknowledgements.

Contents

The Air Wars in Context

The history of the Twentieth century has been profoundly affected by its two great wars, and this fact is reflected in the literature of the time. Our often-times horrified fascination with war, and with emotions and responses of those caught up in it, has been a fertile source for both fiction and non-fiction. In the Canadian context of the First World War, for example, the motivations of a generation which felt itself compelled to enlist and fight in what was essentially a foreign war, has long been rich grist for the mill of novelists. Canadian writers such as Timothy Findlay (*The Wars*), Hugh McClennan (*Barometer Rising*), and Michael Ondaatje (*The English Patient*) have attempted to explore and contextualize these feelings. they move their narratives in effect, beyond mere facts, and instead attempt to recapture some piece of the human event itself.

Novelists, however, are free to manipulate plots, as well as to create a con-textualing setting against which they develop their characters actions. Ironically, no such contextualing information surrounds recollections of actual historical events. The appeal of fiction lies in its ability to answer all our questions as it moves to a dramatically definable climax. It is not necessary to understand the conditions under which soldiers fought and all to often died to enjoy a work of fiction. The novelist will provide us with the necessary clues and additional information we need.

The historian, on the other hand, is doubly hampered. First, he or she can only report the truth, as determined by the examination of the evidence, coupled with interviews and reports. Secondly, he or she must attempt to convey the surrounding context against which these events played themselves out. In the case of the air war fought in the First and Second World Wars, this task becomes Herculean.

The years that separate us from these two wars have seen a virtual explosion of technology. Aircraft today that fly at great altitudes are routinely pressurized, and even the most frequent flyer has little inkling of what it felt like to fly and fight in the aircraft of the World Wars. As such, it is often as difficult for us to imagine fighting a war from the wicker seat of a Great war biplane, or the noisy cold inside a second World War bomber, as it is to imagine fighting alongside

Wolf at Quebec, or against Perry on Lake Erie. In fact, given the recent popularity of re-enactment societies, as well as the resurgence of interest in 'Tall ships', the average person is far more likely to have a nodding acquaintance with these events than with the aerial battles of the first and second World Wars.

It is precisely for these reasons that a book such as *Canada's Fighting Pilots* is so useful. Edmond Cosgrove has written an eloquent testimony to the remarkable heroism displayed by Canadian pilots in both the First and Second World Wars. Gathering together the stories of some of Canada's greatest pilots, it is a classic in its field, and takes us directly into the world of aerial combat in the two world wars.

Canada's Fighting Pilots outlines the exploits of such legendary figures as: William "Billy" Bishop; whose daring, solo dawn raid on a German airfield won him the Victoria Cross; William Barker; who fought single-handedly an entire squadron of enemy aircraft; George "Buzz" Beurling, the ace of Malta who achieved a remarkable score of victories fighting from an island under siege; Andrew Mynarski, whose attempts to save the life of a trapped comrade, high over Germany, ultimately cost him his own. The original author, a longtime CBC broadcaster, has written the book in a winning and entertaining manner that is still clear to the non-aviation enthusiast.

This latest treatment preserves all of Cosgrove's style and attention to detail. What it hopes to add is information about these times and events that would no longer be common knowledge to the average reader. As a former pilot with intimate knowledge of these now vintage aircraft, I know firsthand how difficult it is to fly and maintain them. Even relatively sophisticated aircraft such as the Spitfire Vc's that George Beurling flew over Malta, would seem hopelessly outdated by today's standards.

Also, most people have no experience with the tactics and maneuvers necessary in aerial combat. Aviation has advanced so much that even modern military pilots would be unfamiliar with combat as it was fought in 1918, or even 1944. Changes in technology, aircraft speed and strength, even something as mundane as the clothing issued to pilots, all contributed to how these air battles were fought.

Great War aerial combat

It is hardly an understatement that the Western Front of World War I was unlike anything seen before or since. Years of unremitting trench warfare had effected a profound change on not only the physical landscape, but on the social one as well. Just as the countryside of France and Belgium had been devastated by the largest bombardments in history, so too had traditional views of warfare been exploded. The earlier enthusiasm that had led such people as Arthur Lowe, a prominent, contemporary Canadian social historian to declare a few years earlier that "A nice little war would be just what the country needed to cap its development and give it a sense of corporate unity" had been tempered by years of casualty lists. Instead, a grim sense of purpose, a feeling to make whatever sacrifices were necessary to end the bloody conflict, prevailed. By the end of the first year of the war, no one was under the illusion that warfare could be considered to be anything other than what it really was: dirty, unglamorous, uncomfortable, and extremely dangerous.

The air war grew out of this world-view. While historians have to a certain extent mythologized Great War pilots as "gallant Knights of the skies," the reality was far different. Films and popular fiction have portrayed World War I pilots as silk-scarved daredevils, clear of eye and firm of spirit. Here, in a particularly egregious example from a post-war biography of Manfred Von Richtofen-the famed 'Red Baron'- this mythologized image can be clearly seen:

> [i]nto this grisly story of World War I there came a refreshing gleam of the chivalry of old, when the pick of the flower of youth on both sides carried the conflict into the skies. Into that Knighthood of the Blue, Richtofen has been given a place of highest merit by those he fought with and against.
>
> His life and death, his victories and defeats, his loves, his hopes, his fears bring a new record to the halls of that same Valhalla in which rests the spirit of... many others who fought aloft and died below with hearts that held emotions other than hate.
>
> young blood, hot and daring, raced through their veins, even as the winged steeds they rode raced on the wind to conquest or disaster With keen young eyes, glinting along the barrels of their jibbering machine guns, they looked at close range into one another's souls as they pressed the triggers that sent one another tumbling down to death.

Clearly, the reality of the life of a service pilot would seem hopelessly pedestrian in comparison to such overblown descriptions. In actuality, aircraft are quite difficult to spot while flying, being reduced to mere specks from only a mile away. When clouds, haze, and other meteorological phenomena are factored in, it is a little known fact that relatively few patrols in either war resulted in combat.

Second World War air combat

In the Second World War many of the lessons from the Great War had to be relearned, not just by individual pilots, but air forces as a whole. Overconfidence in the ability of aircraft to defend themselves, or to avoid combat altogether, led to terrible losses in all air forces initially. It quickly became apparent that in the deadly arena of air combat only high-speed, high powered, and well-armed aircraft would survive.

The Supermarine Spitfire was such an aircraft. Originally derived from an air-racing seaplane — powerful, nimble and formidably armed — the Spitfire was the ideal aircraft to defend the tiny, but strategic, Mediterranean island of Malta. A pure interceptor, the machine gun and cannon armed Spitfire was also equipped with a two-stage supercharger, giving it a crucial margin of power in the thin air above the island. While lacking in range (a feature never envisioned by its creator Reginald Mitchell) the Spitfire went through a number of wartime modifications and upgrades. It is telling that the Spitfire was the only Commonwealth aircraft that flew operationally on both the first and last day of the war.

Commonwealth bombers, by contrast faced a much different task. Their primary mission was to carry the war to the enemy, in the form of bombing raids. Unfortunately, heavy losses during daylight raids forced Commonwealth bombers to operate under cover of darkness. German night fighters, aided by the first primitive radar sets, prowled among the bomber streams unseen, decimating formations. Here instead of speed, the emphasis was on robustness and power. Bombers were protected in-flight by air-gunners; aircrew sitting inside electrically operated turrets and manning banks of machine guns. All to often, however, these electrically operated turrets would fail if an aircraft took battle damage. Moreover, it was physically demanding to fly and fight from inside aircraft in both wars.

Environmental concerns and air combat

Passengers flying in today's modern airliners have little idea of what a hostile environment lies on the other side of their seat side window. The arrow straight, picturesque trails left in a jet's wake, for example, (commonly known as condensation trials, or 'contrails') are actually the result of the hot engine exhaust gasses freezing in the subzero air; a cold that is exacerbated by the wind from the aircraft's slipstream (passage through the air). Crouched behind a tiny windscreen, or stuffed into a tiny, metal turret, pilots and aircrew alike suffered from near debilitating cold at high altitude, even on the warmest of summer days. Aircrews combated this by wearing bulky fur-lined flying clothing, but this in turn severely restricted their range of motion, at a time when it was sorely needed. Indeed, it is worth noting that during World War II, most fighter pilots rarely wore their large sheepskin 'Irvin' jackets while flying. The bulk of the jacket, especially when worn under a life jacket, parachute and seat harnesses, was far too constrictive for combat. Similar restrictions in bombers resulted in aircrews wearing only their parachute harness, the parachute itself being clipped on in an emergency.

Engine vibration, often quite severe in Great War aircraft, could rapidly bring on pilot fatigue and cramping. Aircraft with rotary engines, in which the engine rotated about a fixed crankshaft, required continuous application of rudder to keep the plane from rolling off to one side. The more sophisticated aircraft of World War II, while somewhat less susceptible to engine vibration, still required considerable effort to move their non-hydraulically assisted controls, especially at high speeds.

Even mundane items such as diet played a role in air combat. Wartime rationing in Britain during World War II lead to reliance upon such vegetables as cabbage and Brussels sprouts as a supplement to aircrew meals. Bomber crews, forced to spend hours at altitude, found the cabbage produced excessive gas in the intestinal tract, leading to severe cramping. Similarly, during the siege of Malta in 1942 rationing of supplies meant that, on average, pilots such as George Beurling were issued three slices of tinned, corned beef (known as 'bully beef' by all), and two slices of bread per day. Pilots were often known to wrap the leftover food in a handkerchief and carry it on their person rather than leave it lying about, a target for any hungry soul. (This diet was often supplemented by two tablespoons of shredded carrot soaked in castor oil.) While not often considered a factor, hunger was frequently as large a concern as enemy activity.

Even when battle was joined, the odds were often heavily against the Canadian pilots. Until late in both World Wars, the Canadians often flew in outdated aircraft and at numerical disadvantages. During the siege of Malta, for example, several aircraft would routinely be sent aloft to face several dozen incoming attackers. First World War aircraft, even the relatively robust S.E.5a, were horribly fragile: being composed of wooden frames covered by fabric made highly flammable through a treatment known as 'doping,' i.e. impregnating the fabric with acetates to make it taut and waterproof. Aircraft in both wars were unpressurized and air combats routinely took place above 10,000 feet, where supplemental oxygen is necessary. It is worth noting that while such oxygen was a standard feature in Second World War aircraft, no Great War aircraft was so equipped.

The mental war in the air

Of course, during the heat of battle pilots would undoubtedly push such discomforts to the back of their mind. While physically demanding, the act of flying an aircraft pales in comparison to the mental gymnastics of air combat. For some people used to a two dimensional battlefield, the war in the air struck many as a type of free-form nightmare. Aircraft could attack from any direction, and there was no such thing as an 'unfair' kill. It was (and still is) extremely challenging to keep track of aircraft during combat maneuvering. Maintaining what is known today as 'situational awareness' during the wild aerobatics of combat would literally be a matter of life or death.

Anyone doubting that air fighting was a grim and deadly serious business should consider the tactics developed by a mentor of Von Richtofen, Oswald Boelke. His "Dicta" became the basis for most of the airfighting in the Great War on both sides. It serves as perhaps the first articulation of air combat strategy:

Boelke's Dicta

1. Secure all possible advantages before attacking.
2. Always carry through an attack once you have started it.
3. Fire only at close range, when your opponent is properly in your sights.
4. Keep your eye on your opponent and never let yourself be deceived by ruses.
5. Always assail your opponent from behind.
6. If your opponent dives on you, do not try to escape but fly to meet it.
7. Never forget your line of retreat.
8. Whenever possible attack in formations of four or six and when the fight breaks up take care that several do not go for the same opponent.

Nearly, forty years later, the British ace A.G. "Sailor" Malan (who, as we will see, served as a commanding officer for George Beurling) expanded upon these rules:

Malan's 10 rules for Air fighting

1. Wait until you see the whites of his eyes. Fire short bursts of one or two seconds, and only when your sites are definitely "ON".
2. Whilst shooting, think of nothing else, brace the whole of your body, have both hands on the stick, concentrate on your ring site.
3. Always keep a sharp lookout. "Keep your finger out!"
4. Height gives you the initiative.
5. Always turn and face the attack.
6. Make your decisions promptly. It is better to act quickly even though your tactics are not the best.
7. Never fly straight and level for more than thirty seconds in the combat area.
8. When diving to attack, always leave a proportion of your formation above to act as top guard.
9. INITIATIVE, AGGRESSION, AIR DISCIPLINE, and TEAMWORK are words that MEAN something in air fighting.
10. Go in quickly - Punch hard - Get out!

It is perhaps a little known fact today, but World War I's famed ace Baron Manfred von Richtofen "the Red Baron" scored most of his victories attacking slower, less heavily armed two seat aircraft, usually from behind.

This book is first and foremost the chronicle of the pilots who fought for Canada and the Commonwealth. Cosgrove ably tells the tale of their exploits, and their heroism. For this reason alone, this book is an important part of the story of Canadian history in general, and military history in particular. Perhaps more importantly, however, it also serves as a window into a world, and a form of combat, that can never be recreated. Modern jet fighter pilots may still have to fight against the crushing onset of G's induced by combat, for example, and air travel can never be rendered absolutely safe and benign. Yet the discomforts, perils, and dangers faced by the pilots described in this book were unique to their particular time and place. By reading their stories, we are transported to a time that, although full of dangers, was also full of wonder and the excitement engendered by any new endeavor. The stories are important, exciting, and, not incidentally, uniquely Canadian.

Selected Bibliography

Beurling, George and Leslie Roberts. (1943). *Malta Spitfire: The Story of a Fighter Pilot*. Toronto: Oxford University Press.

Bishop, William A. (1975). *Winged Warfare*. London: Pan Books.

Bishop, William Arthur. (1965). *The Courage of the Early Morning: A Son's biography of a Famous Father*. Toronto: McClelland & Stewart.

Bowen, Ezra. (1980). *Knights of the Air*. Chicago: Time-Life Books.

Bower, Chaz. (1993). *For Valour: The Air VC's*. London: William Kimber.

Lewis, Bruce. (1996). *A Few of the First: The Story of the Royal Flying Corps & the Royal Naval Air Service in the First World War*. Haverton, PA: Casemate.

Lucas, Laddie. (1992). *Malta: The Thorn in Rommel's side*. London: Penguin.

McCaffery, Dan. (1988). *Billy Bishop: Canadian Hero*. Toronto: James Lorimar & Company, Ltd.

Morgan, Eric and Edward Shacklady. (1960). *Spitfire: The History*. Stamford, Lincolnshire: Key Books Ltd.

Page, Betty (Editor). (1996). *Mynarski's Lanc : The Story of Two Famous Canadian Lancaster Bombers KB726 & FM213*. Boston: Boston Mills Press.

Ralph, Wayne. (1999). *Barker VC: The Classic Story of a Legendary First World War Hero*. London: Grub Street Press.

Roberts, Leslie. (1959). *There Shall be Wings: A History of the Royal Canadian Air Force*. Toronto: Clarke Irwin & Company Ltd.

Robertson, Bruce. (1960). *Spitfire: The Story of a Famous Fighter*. Fallbrook, California: Aero Publishing Inc.

Shores, Christopher. (1975). *Fighter Aces*. London: Hamlyn Publishing Group.

Shores, Christopher and Brian Cull. (1991). *Malta: The Spitfire Year 1942*. London: Grub Street Press.

Wise, Sydney F. (1980). *Canadian Airmen and the First World War: The Official History of the Royal Canadian Air Force, Volume I*. Toronto: University of Toronto Press.

Not to the glory of war, but to the
Canadians who inherit these heroic
legends of valour and devotion to duty.

Acknowledgements (to the 1965 edition)

Without the countless snippets of fact given me by a great many persons, this book could not hope to be an accurate account of the men with whom it is concerned. The official records give only the barest of outlines and source books can be inaccurate.

In particular, I am indebted to Air Vice-Marshal McEwen for him invaluable assistance and advice. John Shaw of the Victoria Daily Colonist suggested the columns from which this book developed, and without his generous support it would not have been written. And for their interest and encouragement in what proved to be a lengthy project I should like to thank Al Cheeseman and R.W.W. Robertson of Clarke, Irwin & Company Limited.

Preface

In writing this penetrating and exciting book, Mr. Cosgrove leads us back unerringly to the early crucial days of aerial combat in World War I, and to the birth of the airplane as a decisive weapon in modern war. From those days, he goes on to describe the outstanding role played by Canadian aviators in World War II when, once again, Canada played a part out of all proportion to the size of her population in the war in the air. Indeed, it is with a feeling akin to awe that we realize that the airmen brought to life by the author are but a small proportion of the vast number of brave flyers of whom Canada can be proud.

To chronicle the events covered by this book as a chain of related facts would have been an achievement in itself; but to view them through the deeds and the personalities of the men who were the central figures lifts this book from the realm of history into the realm of true adventure. It servers to remind us, furthermore, that until somebody can devise a machine that will substitute in every way for the human brain and, what is perhaps more important, for the human spirit, there can be no replacement in any high endeavour for the sort of men who fill the pages of Mr. Cosgrove's book.

For me, and for all who have served and are serving in the Royal Canadian Air Force, this volume must hold a special significance. To us the gallery of heroes from Barker to Beurling is more than a collection of unusual men; these men are the foundation upon which the Royal Canadian Air Force was built. And the strength of the Air Force today is attributable in large measure to the pride in service that was created by those who transformed the first flimsy machines into winged chariots.

I am sure that the exploits recounted in this book will inspire not only those of us whose memories span the few short years that have witnessed the fantastic growth of air power, but also the young men of today on whose shoulders will rest the responsibility of carrying the airplane and the space capsule beyond the new frontiers.

Hugh Campbell
Air Marshal

The Background

In July, 1940, Adolph Hitler's dream of a Nazi Europe was swiftly becoming a reality. Poland, Denmark, Norway, Holland, Belgium, France-all had fallen victim to a new concept in warfare, the *Blitzkrieg*, or "lightning war." The German victories had been triumphs of science over tradition. While the Allied forces were being deployed in the manner of the First World War, Hitler's armies, headed by fast-moving, armoured Panzer divisions, were advancing smoothly over the desolation laid by the far-ranging bombers of Germany's air force, and ripping the static defence systems of the Allies to shreds. With the fall of France only Britain was left to face the German military machine across the twenty-two miles of the English Channel. Now faint vapour trails, like smoky fingers in the sky, pointed ominously towards England: once more the planes of the Luftwaffe were spearheading the advance of Hitler's legions.

Hitler and his generals had realized that the great speed, range, and firepower of airplanes made them decisive factors in modern warfare. The key to success in war was air supremacy. While the Allied forces were still using planes as back-up auxiliaries of the infantry, German planes were smashing defence lines and cities into helplessness, leaving them easy prey for the conquering Panzer and infantry divisions. The German generals were certain that the same smashing blows of the Luftwaffe would pave the way for the conquest of Britain.

For the safe Channel crossing of the German tanks, armoured cars, and soldiers, protection from British air attack was essential. Therefore, the first step in Hitler's plan of conquest was the destruction of the RAF. Hermann Goering, Commander-in-Chief of the Luftwaffe, promised Hitler that he would crush the RAF. His pilots would ruthlessly destroy the enemy's flying fields, aircraft factories, and training schools. With the RAF wiped out, the German armada would cross the Channel unhindered and land in a defenceless England.

Britain's chances of turning back the invaders seemed slim. Now that Germany had met and crushed the most powerful armies in Western Europe, most observers believed, like the American ambassador to London, Joseph P. Kennedy, father of the late President, that Britain did not stand "a Chinaman's chance" of surviving. All during the 1930's, while Germany had been building its modern military machine, Britain had maintained fleets of obsolete planes, tanks, and ships. After the evacuation from Dunkirk the RAF had rebuilt feverishly in an attempt to make up the deficit, but when the first, probing attacks of the Luftwaffe hit the island nation the RAF could muster only 700 operational fighter planes. Against these 700, Germany, in July, 1940, launched an overwhelming force of 3,000 first-line fighters and bombers, and the Battle of Britain began.

It was a grim death struggle. The outnumbered RAF pilots carried out as many as ten missions a day, flying until they were exhausted and withdrawing from the fight only when their planes were damaged or they themselves were wounded. Every day the German formations hurled themselves at RAF installations. These tactics had spelled success in Poland, the Low Countries, and France. But against Britain the offensive was a costly one, for the British fighter pilots were aided by a massive radar network that pinpointed the invading bomber fleets even as they assembled over occupied France. The Germans suffered losses of two to one. Nevertheless, their overwhelming numbers began to take their toll and Germany was on the verge of victory when, unexpectedly, Hitler switched his attacks from the RAF installations to London. This change in German tactics, which saved the RAF from annihilation, was the result of a bold counter-stroke by the British. During the height of the attack on their installations, RAF night bombers bombarded several cities in Germany. The Nazi leaders had promised the people of Germany that no enemy bomb should fall on German cities and the British raids so infuriated Hitler that he diverted the Luftwaffe from its primary task of destroying British air power and ordered it to punish British cities in retaliation. Now huge formations of German bombers, escorted by fighters, bombarded the city of London, thus beginning the second phase of the Battle of Britain.

The respite from the attack on its bases gave the RAF a chance to replace its losses. As Fighter Command recovered strength, huge air battles were fought over London and south-east England, and Hitler was forced to change his tactics yet again. This time the German bombers arrived under the protective shroud of darkness and were very difficult to detect, even with the aid of radar. Through the twilight of autumn, and on into the winter, the German attacks grew in fury. The industrial centres of Coventry, Birmingham, and Leeds shared with London the ordeal of lying helpless under the fearful rain of bombs from the night skies. The climax of the Blitz came on the night of December 29, 1940, when incendiary bombs started 1,500 separate fires, and London knew the second Great Fire of her history.

But the bravery of those in the cities was matched by the British pilots in the air. Again and again RAF fighters hurled themselves with desperate courage against the attacking waves of bombers. Under the hammering blows of the RAF the German attacks gradually faltered. Finally they ceased. The great scheme for the conquest of Britain had been overthrown; Hitler was forced to turn eastward to his other great enemy, the Soviet Union.

For the first time in history air power alone had determined the course of an entire war. It was the RAF that had thrown out Hitler's timetable of conquest and saved Britain. In the British House of Commons Prime Minister Winston Churchill paid tribute to the gallantry of the men in the slender Spitfires and needle-nosed Hurricanes when he said "Never, in the field of human conflict, was so much owed by so many to so few."

In their courage and heroism the fighter pilots of the Battle of Britain were continuing a cherished tradition that went back to the First World War. Remembering the legends that had emerged from those first years of combat flying, the pilots of the Second World War felt themselves to be something special from the start, with much to live up to. The fighter pilot was one of the elite one of the bravest and most daring. His initiative and imagination, combined with iron nerves and lightning reflexes, were essential in surviving the hazards of combat flying.

In the First World War pilots had to possess luck as well as daring. Airplanes then were frail, ungainly collections of wings, struts, and wires, liable to fall into a spin at the least gust of wind, and powered by engines that often conked out for no apparent reason. Bouncing along at eighty to ninety miles an hour, they faced the universal wrath of all ground troops, whether friend or foe, who fired indiscriminately at any flying machine that came their way. "Flying bedsteads" the pilots called them; and sometimes, "flying coffins."

In 1914 the airplane was considered by military authorities to be little more than a temperamental toy. However, army chiefs on both sides conceded that it had some value for spying out the movements of enemy forces, and each army corps was provided with a few flying machines for this purpose. Reconnaissance missions were traditionally the task of the cavalry, but mud, trenches, and the deadly fire of machine guns had immobilized this arm of the service, and more and more the airplane became the eyes of the army. The hard-pressed pilots, many of them in fact ex-cavalrymen, carried out their dangerous work conscientiously, often after only the most rudimentary training. With smoke bombs, flares, and wireless telegraphy they signalled valuable information about the movements of the enemy. They even began a campaign of harassing enemy troops.

Flying under such conditions, it is understandable that opposing pilots exchanged nothing more than courteous waves when they passed, each intent on handling his machine and spying out the movements of the other's ground forces. But as the months wore on, and the flying and the planes improved, pilots began to exchange more than greetings. They began taking pistols, rifles, hand grenades, and even bricks into the air with them. These rudimentary missiles were sometimes effective and once in a while a British, French, or German plane would spin into the ground, victim, of a well-placed bullet. Yet even this was only a token of hostility, and for the most part a pilot could pursue his reconnaissance mission without much thought for the enemy planes that buzzed past him.

Then, in 1915, a French aviator named Roland Garros fastened metal shields to the propeller of his plane, bolted a machine gun on the cowling, and revolutionized aerial warfare. With the primitive protective strips on the propeller, Garros could now fire a machine gun through the spinning arc, and his plane became, in effect, a flying gun. In sixteen days he shot down five German planes, winning himself the adulation of the French press and the title "ace flyer." Garros's device was too primitive to last though. On one patrol, the impact of the bullets striking the metal shields caused his motor to shake loose on its mounting, and he was forced to land behind German lines. His plane was seized before he could burn it and the secret was out. Germany called in one of its top aircraft designers, Anthony Fokker, to study the Garros invention. In less than forty-eight hours Fokker had devised an improvement that regulated the rate of fire so that a pilot could shoot through the arc of a propeller without striking the blades. From this beginning, aerial combat was born, and flying, dangerous enough in the primitive machines of 1915, became doubly hazardous for Allied airmen, who were now forced to patrol skies dominated by well-armed Fokker fighters. The wood and canvas planes were highly vulnerable to machine gun fire, and parachutes were still a thing of the future. But this did little to daunt the trail-blazing combat flyers. Allied pilots quickly armed their planes with machine guns to counter the Fokker menace. A new phase in the history of aviation was beginning.

The value of aerial reconnaissance flights, conducted by two-seater planes, was now well established — so much so that a counter-weapon had to be created. The fighter plane was developed: a machine designed to carry only one man, whose sole purpose was to destroy enemy observation planes. This man had to possess certain definite characteristics. While all flyers needed a spirit of adventure coupled with a certain disregard for personal safety, the pilots of these new pursuit planes had first and foremost to be fighters. These aerial gladiators were often compared with knights of old. To a public sickened by the mud and slaughter of the battlefields, the war in the air offered, a glimpse of the fame and glory once expected of war. The flyer was glamorized by war correspondents as a twentieth-century knight errant, and he lived up to his reputation. In 1916, aerial chivalry reached its full flower. The knights were now fully armed: their lances were the fiery tracer bullets fired from their speeded-up machine guns; their steeds were contraptions which, though primitive by modern standards, were mettlesome enough for the task before them.

As in the days of chivalry, these knights of the air developed their own code of honour. It was inconceivable to shoot down an opponent whose guns had jammed or whose motor had failed. Explosive bullets, which caused terrible, non-healing wounds, were considered the weapons of a coward. And just as the knights rode into battle on gaily caparisoned steeds, their shields emblazoned with family crests and their helmets sporting bright plumes, so the fighter pilots of 1916 painted their aircraft bizarre colours, with their own personal insignia on the fuselage. For identification purposes coloured streamers fluttered from the helmets and wing struts of the flight leaders.

It was a romantic form of warfare, but most of these young officers were former cavalrymen, and the fashionable cavalry regiments of Europe had only recently laid aside the sabre, lance, and duelling sword for more modern weapons. Consequently, opposing flyers often challenged each other to jousts and tournaments to determine the most skilled warrior. Yet even as the code of chivalry was being formed it was becoming obsolete. The tempo of the war increased as the weapons improved, and it was no longer merely a matter of who was the better warrior. Airplanes were being called upon for deadlier tasks.

Formations increased in size and aircraft were given more significant tactical and strategic roles to play. They battled their way to targets far behind enemy lines and bombarded key railroad centres and ammunition depots. Strategic bombing of industrial targets came into being as early as 1916, when a formation of Royal Navy Sopwith two-seaters penetrated deep into Germany to bomb an arms factory. It was the first manifestation of air power as a strategic weapon, and it is a source of pride to Canada that many of the flyers who took part in this pioneer raid were Canadians.

Men from all over the Commonwealth joined the daredevil brotherhood of combat flyers in World War I. Since none of the Dominions yet possessed its own air force (Canada formed hers just as the war was ending), aspiring young Commonwealth flyers joined the RAF. In 1917 one squadron in action on the western front included in its twenty pilots men from Britain, Australia, New Zealand, South Africa, Canada, and even a warrior from India, who flew into battle wearing a turban in place of the regulation leather flying helmet. Of all these young adventurers, the wildest and bravest were widely acknowledged to be the Canadians. It was a Canadian who first looped his French-made Nieuport to shoot down an opponent. Canadians flew on every type of mission with such courage and skill that the belief grew that they were born to fly. Their duties carried them into the skies of France, Italy, Macedonia, East Africa, and Turkey, and over the North Sea, the Red Sea, and the Indian Ocean. In passing they left a record of daring and devotion that was famous everywhere. Canadian aviation won a total of 495 decorations for valour during the First World War, including three coveted Victoria Crosses. Of the twenty-seven RAF pilots in World War I to achieve the distinction of destroying more than thirty enemy aircraft, eleven were Canadians. Of the ten leading aces in the formative years of the Royal Air Force, five were Canadians.

During the Second World War this tradition of Canadian excellence in combat flying was revived, and four hundred Canadian airmen shared the danger and glory of the Battle of Britain. In bombers, as well as fighters, Canadians earned their reputation. Before World War II ended, as many as forty squadrons of various types carried the colours of the RCAF to all theatres of the far-flung conflict, while Canada itself became the centre of the greatest training scheme in the history of aviation, the Commonwealth Air Training Plan.

It took many hundreds of Canadian flyers to set and maintain these high standards of achievement, and it would be impossible to name every one of them. But there are some winged giants of both wars whose exploits make them stand out before all others. These are men such as Beurling and Bishop, McLaren and McEwen, Barker and Collishaw. This is their story.

"The Greatest of Them All"

The two seater reconnaissance planes of early 1916 were slow, cumbersome machines, easy prey for the faster, better-armed fighters. Many a fighter pilot ran up an impressive score of victories by confining his attacks to such cold meat targets. The pilot of a marauding Fokker which dived out of the sun one day had this aim in mind when he attacked the RFC plane carrying Bill Barker in the observation cockpit. Minutes later the Fokker was a tangled wreck on the battlefield below. Reacting to the threat, Barker had promptly swivelled his Lewis machine gun around and met the charging German plane with a searing fusillade of bullets. It was Bill Barker's first victory, and the pilots of No. 9 Squadron looked on the newly arrived gravel cruncher, their term for an infantry-man, with new respect.

Barker, a native of Dauphin, Manitoba, had transferred to the Royal Flying Corps from the cavalry after it had bogged down in the mud of Flanders. He was twenty-one years old. It was typical of his personality that he had originally chosen the cavalry, a branch of the service committed, at least in theory, to the role of an attack force. Before long his exploits in the RFC as an observer and his ability with a machine gun earned him a Military Cross and a battlefield promotion to the rank of second lieutenant.

During one patrol over the German lines Barker was hit by a steel splinter from an exploding shell. The wound was painful and he was urged to go to the hospital, but at this time the heavy air fighting of the Battle of the Somme was raging, and the British forces were heavily engaged. Serious casualties had left the squadron under strength, and Barker felt he was needed at the front. Instead of becoming a hospital patient, he asked the squadron doctor merely to bandage the wound. The next day he was back in the air.

Barker served with three different observation squadrons before applying for permission to take flight training as a pilot. The Royal Flying Corps was suffering from an acute pilot shortage at this time. Hundreds of men had been lost during "Bloody April" of 1916, when fast new German aircraft swept the skies of France.

Maj. William G. Barker in RAF uniform.
Swaine/National Archives of Canada/PA-122516

In November, 1916, Barker was sent to the flying school at Narborough, England. The young Canadian had already learned much about flying during his days as an observer. He had pestered his pilots to teach him the fundamentals of flying and had on occasion tried his hand at the controls. This private instruction paid dividends at Narborough, for after only one hour of dual instruction an astonished instructor told him he was ready to solo: "There's nothing I can teach you. You're a born pilot."

By January, 1917, Barker had completed his training and, with a new pair of pilot's wings stitched to his tunic, he was assigned to No. 15 Observation Squadron at the front. He was given command of C Flight and promoted to the rank of captain. This, however, was not quite the assignment Barker had wanted. During training at Narborough, the touch of the control stick and the response of the aircraft had been heady wine for the young Canadian. He had hoped to be posted to a fighter squadron. But a higher authority had considered his experience and had decided he would be more valuable in observation work.

The slow-moving RE-8 two-seaters flown by No. 15 Squadron promised Barker little opportunity to indulge in the aerobatics he had come to love during training, and even less chance to take part in the aerial duels that were the daily lot of fighter pilots. But at least his new job was action, and he was glad to be back in the battle area. He brought to his assignments all the determination and accuracy he had displayed as an observer. Day after day he flew the creaky old RE-8 low over enemy positions, spotting troop movements and selecting targets for the British artillery. On one mission Barker's keen eyes picked out the signs of an impending enemy attack. He relayed his information by wireless back to his artillery, and a British bombardment broke up the attack before it could jump off. Barker's alertness earned him a bar to his Military Cross, the equivalent of winning the medal twice. Barker's knowledge of front line flying had by this time attracted the attention of his superiors, and it was decided that he could help the war effort better by passing this knowledge on to others. Barker was assigned to a flying school in England as an instructor.

His immediate reaction was to apply through "proper channels" for reassignment back to a front line unit. After three such requests failed to produce the desired results, the young flyer rebelled in his characteristic manner. Using the transparent excuse of teaching fledgling pilots the intricacies of fighter aerobatics, Barker barnstormed over the quiet English countryside like a one-man flying circus. He flew at almost zero altitudes, hedgehopping over barns and buildings and executing snap rolls and stall turns that sent chills down the spines of the staff of the flying school. He capped his performance with a power dive over a nearby Army headquarters that all but lifted the shingles from the roof. After several days of this his superiors had had enough. It was either a court martial or a transfer for this crazy Canadian, and, since good pilots were in short supply, it was decided to send Barker back to France. Then began in earnest one of the most spectacular careers in military aviation.

Tactics had changed in the aerial war when Barker returned to France. If 1916 had been the age of chivalry, when opposing pilots pursued their quarries with almost knightlike courtesy, 1917 was the year of the fighter squadron. Air fighting had become a battle to the death, with both sides mounting larger and larger aerial formations in the relentless effort to sweep the foe from the skies. This development had led to giant air battles, or dogfights, in which the solo duellist of 1916 had no place.

In the earlier months of 1917 German air power had been in the ascendancy. Newer types of aircraft, notably the Albatros D-5 and the Fokker Triplane, had allowed German airmen to duplicate the conditions of "Bloody April," 1916. As the summer passed into autumn, however, newer British and French models such as the Sopwith Camel, the SE-5 Scout and the French-made Spad tended to balance out this unequal contest.

Bill Barker returned to France in the autumn of 1917 as a flight commander with No. 28 Army Co-operation Squadron, a newly organized unit equipped with the temperamental little Sopwith Camel. The Squadron was based at Droglandt just behind the village of Poperinghe in the Ypres Salient. The Salient, an unnatural bulge into the German-held line, had been created in 1914 when Allied troops had courageously blocked the advance of the Prussian Guards in the First Battle of Ypres. Six months later, in the Second Battle of Ypres, Canada's First Division won immortality by holding the line for almost two weeks against more than a dozen German divisions equipped with deadly poison gas. Over a period of less than three years this patch of land was drenched with the blood of more than a million men.

The Third Battle of Ypres was almost spent when No. 28 Squadron arrived at the battlefront in October, 1917. At first there was little to do, since heavy rains had flooded the battlefield and effectively blocked any further ground offensive. During brief spells of clear skies, pilots of the new squadron made quick sight-seeing trips over the lines to become familiar with the terrain.

For Barker, the enforced leisure was not wasted. He was busy discovering new things about the Camel. The tiny fighter was a moody little machine that required a soft touch on the controls. Stubby, broad-winged, and, small even by contemporary standards, the Sopwith Camel was powered by a rotary engine, so that all its cylinders were mounted radially. The entire engine, along with the propeller, revolved around a stationary crankshaft. The result was a vicious torque action which made the plane liable to fall into a right-hand spin if the pilot was careless. More than one Camel pilot was killed simply through making a righthand turn after take-off, for then the plane, still climbing and near stalling speed, fell into a sharp spin from which no pilot could recover.

On the positive side, the Camel was the first British fighter to mount two forward-firing Vickers .303 machine guns synchronized to fire through the arc of the propeller. This armament placed it on an even footing with existing German fighters. Moreover, some of its apparent faults were blessings in disguise. The Camel's short fuselage and broad wings made it extremely manoeuvrable at low altitudes, and the gyroscopic action of the motor enabled it literally to "turn on a dime," a feature which endeared it to many a British pilot who found a German fighter riding his tail.

After he had made a thorough study of the features of his new plane, Barker offered a revolutionary theory of air fighting. The accepted dogma of combat flying was then, and still is, that speed plus height equals success. The pilot who dived on his opponent from superior altitude, boosting the speed of his aircraft with the gravitational pull of a power dive, could make a pass with guns blazing and swoop away to safety. Barker realized that the Camel, powered with a 110-horsepower engine, could not hope to match the faster German Albatros fighter which was equipped with 160- and 200-horsepower motors. But he noted that the fastdiving, heavy German fighter made poor dive recovery and, unlike the Camel, failed to respond quickly to the controls at low altitudes.

Barker suggested to his wingmates that the Camel's principal fault, the torque action created by the motor, could be turned to advantage. His theory fell on deaf ears, for most pilots were reluctant to gamble away precious altitude in what could be a fatal experiment. Boldly, Barker decided to put his theory to the test.

He practised contour flying with his Camel; that is, flying as close to the earth as possible, rising and falling with the contours of the ground. As he had expected, the new plane hugged the ground beautifully. He concluded from these experiments that, in certain circumstances, the little Camel was a better plane than the Albatros.

Clearing weather soon gave him a chance to test his theory. In the final week of October, 1917, Barker, accompanied by two companions, Lieutenants Malik and Fenton, went hunting over the German lines. There was no shortage of targets. for the brightening skies brought German patrols up in force. Just over the German lines a flight of seven of the faster Albatros fighters passed beneath the three Camels, and Barker led his companions into the attack. This was the chance he had waited for: an opportunity to prove the Camel's superiority over the more powerful German fighter. As the German formation split wide open to avoid the diving Camels, Barker found himself paired off against an enemy pilot whose evasive action proved he was no novice. While fencing for an opening, Barker deliberately lost altitude, luring his opponent closer and closer to the ground with enticing views of the Camel in the ring sight of the German's Spandau guns. At less than 1,500 feet, Barker decided it was time for the final test. The German plane had dodged into a lethal position above and behind him and was diving flat out to close the range between them. It was now or never. Barker tilted his tiny plane up on one wing and whipped it around in a tight right-hand turn. The heavier German plane shot past, its pilot fighting the control stick in a frantic bid to lift the plane's sluggish nose from the dive. In a split second, Barker completed his turn and dropped on the tail of the German. Now the position was reversed and bullets poured into the wings, cockpit, and fuel tank of the Albatros.

Barker had only a fleeting glimpse of the crash, for tracer bullets ripped past his right wing: another German had dropped onto his tail. Heading for the ground, Barker waited until the second German had steepened his dive, then, in exactly the same fashion, he spun around onto the tail of the Albatros. Again flame burst from the punctured fuel tank and the German plane crashed a short distance from the first.

In less than five minutes, Barker had defeated two of the most feared enemy aircraft on the western front. Putting his plane into a climb, he found that the rest of the German formation had fled. The story of the fight passed quickly through the Salient and veteran squadrons began to look up to No. 28.

This imaginative experiment was only one of Barker's innovations in aerial battle tactics. Since air fighting was in its infancy, the hard and fast rules of the business were only then being made, and Barker was among the foremost originators of his day. A quarter of a century later, Canadian pilots of the RCAF would put his theory into practice again. In specially built Spitfires, they were to use the same tactics to lure the high-flying Focke-Wulf 190 down from its vantage point in the clouds to low altitudes where the superiority of the more powerful German engine was offset by the greater manoeuvrability of the Spitfire.

On October 29, 1917, a mud-spattered motorcycle screeched to a halt outside the shack that served as headquarters for No. 28 Squadron. The weary dispatch rider pushed back his goggles, wiped the chalky mud from his face, and grinned at the assortment of mechanics and clerks lounging near the entrance: "Saddle up boys! You're off for sunny Italy."

The squadron had been in action on the western front for less than three weeks, but already it was classed as a veteran unit. During the daily fighting that raged above the battlefield, its pilots had been pitted against the best of the German Air Force. They had received their baptism of fire on the toughest battlefront in France, and many of them had achieved their first victories against veteran German pilots. They had also had losses. More than a third of the squadron's pilots had become casualties. New men took their places, though, and when the orders came to move to Italy, the squadron was at full strength. Britain could ill afford to lose a veteran unit from the Flanders front at this time, but the situation in Italy was desperate. The Austrian army had been reinforced by German divisions withdrawn from the stalemated Flanders front, and from Russia where the war had been ended by the Bolshevik Revolution. The powerful Austro-German force had smashed the Italian army at Caporetto and poured unchecked onto the plains of Lombardy. In the headlong retreat the Italians had lost 800,000 men killed, wounded, and captured. The country tottered on the brink of defeat.

To save the situation, Britain and France were forced to strip their own hard-pressed armies of men, guns, and planes and send them to Italy. Five British divisions were loaded aboard troop trains and rushed through the tunnels of the Alps to the crumbling Italian front.

Within hours of receiving the orders, No. 28 Squadron's riggers, mechanics, and armourers began the monumental task of dismantling their aircraft and loading them, along with the planes of four other RFC squadrons, on flatcars bound for Italy. The five squadrons, now known collectively as VII Brigade, set up shop in fields along the Piave River, the natural water barrier which had helped check the advancing Austrian and German armies after the disaster at Caporetto. The fields had been hastily cleared of brambles and deep grass to provide an even landing strip for the planes. Workshops and hangars, like huge circus tents, were erected, providing minimum protection from the weather for the men and planes. The hard-working ground crew began to reassemble the aircraft and within forty-eight hours No. 28 Squadron had signalled Brigade Headquarters that it was ready for action.

The squadron was based at Grossa, where it shared the flying field with No. 34 Squadron. These two units carried out the first offensive operation of the RFC on the Italian front on November 28, 1917. Because of their keen desire for action, Bill Barker and members of his flight made the first contact with the enemy. High over the Austrian lines, Barker led three companions into action against a formation of five Albatros fighters. Barker sent one of the blackcrossed planes plunging towards the earth in a steep, out-of-control dive from 10,000 feet, then turned his guns on a second Austrian craft. Vickers bullets smashed into the enemy fighter and Barker's companions saw the right wing crumple and fold back along the fuselage.

The victory firmly established Barker's place as the leading fighter pilot of No. 28 Squadron. In a unit that prided itself on its aggressive spirit, Barker was recognized as the foremost exponent of the attack philosophy. And for him, the best way to prove the value of that philosophy was to record the greatest number of victories possible. He became insistent in his victory claims. It was not enough for him to be credited with the "probable" destruction of an enemy aircraft. For this reason he began to experiment with a camera gun, the forerunner of the wing cameras of the Second World War. "He rigged up the camera on his plane near the guns," related fellow pilot "Black Mike" McEwen. "The idea was, he would snap the shutter at the same time that his bullets hit the enemy. But what with trying to fly the plane, trigger his guns and trip the camera shutter all at the same time, it was just too much to do." Barker abandoned the idea of the camera gun, but on December 3, 1917, he demonstrated to his flight members how a determined and aggressive pilot could use daring to triumph against superior odds.

That morning Barker led seven other Camels deep into enemy territory. They had been assigned as the escort to a formation of RE-8 observation planes. The escort. job proved to be uneventful, for the Austrian and German fighters wisely chose to ignore this well-armed armada. After seeing the observation planes safely home, Barker led his Camels back across the enemy lines. He was spoiling for a fight. If the enemy would not come to him, he would have to go to them. To maintain surprise, Barker led his Camels down to 500 feet and, with the rest of the flight strung out behind him, swept across the Piave River to where an

Austrian observation balloon swung lazily at the end of its cable. These captive balloons were probably the best form of aerial observation available to artillery batteries in the First War. Trailing a basket that carried one or two men linked to the ground by telephone cables, the balloons provided a much more stable platform for observing enemy troop movements than the rear cockpit of an observation plane. From his basket, suspended as high as 1,000 feet above his own lines, the balloon observer could look right into the back yard of an opposing army, and spot artillery concentrations, troop movements, and other vital information. When the fat sausages soared into the air, soldiers cowered in their trenches, for they knew that any movement on their part could be seen by the high-flying observer and would mean heavy artillery fire on their trench. Because of this, balloons were always considered prime objectives for fighters. They were certainly inviting targets. Filled with highly inflammable gas, they exploded into flame when hit by incendiary bullets. The observers were equipped with parachutes and their orders were to bail out in the event of attack. The balloons were not undefended, however. Above them were protective patrols of fighters,

Undated image shows a Fokker D.VII fighter on the flight line. The D.VII was derived from the V.11, hands-down winner of a German military competition for one-seat scout planes in Jan. 1918. 400 D.VIIs were ordered from Fokker Flugzeug Werke and more from Albatros, the type reached the Western Front in April 1918 and about 700 had been delivered by the Armistice -- when all examples of the sturdy, nimble and deadly D.VII were specifically ordered surrendered under the Treaty of Versailles. Anthony Fokker, however, smuggled components of about 120 D.VIIs to the Netherlands, where the type remained in production into the 1920s. Powered by the 160-hp Mercedes D.III six-cylinder, water-cooled engine, the D.VII had top speed of 117 mph at 3,280 ft., service ceiling of 19,685 ft., and endurance of 90 minutes. With the 185-hp BMW III, performance was slightly improved. The D.VII was 22 ft. 9 3/4 in.long, spanned 29 ft. 2 1/3 in., stood 9 ft. 1/4 in. high and weighed a maximum 1,984 lb. on takeoff. It carried one pilot and two 7.92 mm LMG 08/15 machine guns.
Department of National Defence/RE-20874-19

while on the ground pre-sighted anti-aircraft guns ringed the balloon with defensive fire through which a low-flying plane had to pass to make an attack.

On that December morning, as Barker sent his plane hurtling at the Austrian gasbag, the observer spotted him and baled out. On the ground, while the winch crews frantically tried to pull the balloon down to safety, antiaircraft gunners swung the muzzles of their machine guns. On his first pass Barker fired about forty rounds, but the bal.. loon failed to take fire. Swinging past in a tight, climbing turn, Barker saw a chilling sight. Intent on watching their flight leader's attack, the other Camels had scattered badly. Now a vari-coloured Albatros D-3, part of the inevitable top cover patrol, had slipped onto the tail of the Camel piloted by Lieutenant S. Waltho, one of Barker's best men. In that moment the balloon was forgotten. Without a wasted movement, Barker kicked his rudder bars and sent the Camel plunging towards the Austrian fighter. Driving the enemy down to 300 feet, like a cowboy herding a steer, he poured bullets into the brightly painted wings and fuselage at point-blank range. The black-crossed fighter fell off on one wing into a vertical dive and burst into flame. Without a pause Barker flipped his plane into a steep bank and bored in on the balloon. A steady stream of bullets ignited the gas and sent the bag flaming to the ground. Down again went the nose of the Camel and, with tracers pouring from his guns, Barker sent A-A gunners and balloon crews scrambling for the safety of the dugouts. A large staff car heading along a nearby road was his next target. Stitching the ground around it with bullets, he sent it crashing into a ditch. Then, his guns empty, he zoomed into the sky, waggled his wings in the signal for the rest of the flight to join up, and headed home.

Barker's one-man offensive had been a graphic demonstration of his attack philosophy. He had shown his flyers the brand of aviator he wanted in his command. He had little patience with the timid or the over-cautious, believing firmly that a pilot on offensive patrol should expend every bullet against the enemy-whether in the air or on the ground before he brought his plane home.

Nevertheless, while Barker displayed a fearless contempt for the bristling defences that surrounded barrage balloons, he never became an ardent balloon-buster. One day he watched a burning, gas-filled sausage, which his bullets had ignited, collapse on top of the parachute of the unarmed observer who baled out at Barker's first pass. The shocking sight was enough for Barker: "I don't fight men who can't fight back," he said grimly. From then on, he refused to attack balloons.

It was a cold, murky Christmas Day in northern Italy when a heavily garbed figure crept silently into the ramshackle building that served as sleeping quarters for No. 28 Squadron. Moving quietly despite the bulky flying gear he wore, Bill Barker shook the shoulders of two sleeping figures. The men snapped awake, dressed quickly, and followed their flight leadef outside. The trio stopped at the mess hall to gulp steaming cups of hot coffee, then walked to the flight line where three Sopwith Camels crouched in the mud, their flat snouts raised to the black northern sky.

Mechanics shivered in the cold as the pilots climbed into the tiny cockpits and began to chant the ritual of starting engines. "Switch off," called the mechanics posted at the nose of each plane. "Switch off," echoed the pilots. The mechanics grasped the heavy wooden propellers with both hands. "Throttle open," they shouted. The pilots echoed the words and the props were swung to suck gasoline into the cylinders. "Throttle closed." Then: "Contact!" The pilots flipped their magneto switches into the "on" position, and the mechanics, poised on one leg, threw their weight against the props in a quick spin. Gasoline flooded the rotary mounted cylinders and the engines coughed into life. At a signal from the pilots, the grease-monkeys pulled the chocks from beneath the wheels and the three Camels lunged forward.

The planes climbed rapidly, despite the extra weight of almost one hundred pounds of bombs that nestled in the racks beneath the fuselage. In a loose V formation, they pointed their whirling propellers north-east. Beneath their wings gunfire flickered in the darkness as they passed over the Piave River battleline.

To the east, the false dawn painted the horizon grey, and the three planes tightened their formation. In the cockpit of the lead ship, Barker huddled his chin deeper into the fleecelined collar of his flying suit, seeking shelter from the bitterly cold wind as he consulted the map strapped to his leg. The sky lightened, revealing snow-covered mountains and valleys. Far below, a troop train sent a cloud of steam into the frosty air as it laboured towards the front. Military traffic cluttered the roads of northern Italy, presenting an inviting target to the three planes skimming overhead.

Barker looked towards the plane on his left, piloted by Lieutenant H. B. Hudson of Victoria, B.C., and gestured with a gloved hand. Hudson peered over the cockpit coaming towards the ground, then nodded vigorously. The pilot of the third plane, on Barker's right, acknowledged his flight leader's signal with a short burst of fire from his machine guns-a necessary precaution before combat in this cold climate, for sometimes the oil in the mechanism froze. Then, one after the other, the planes tipped up on one wing and peeled off into an almost vertical dive.

The rising note of the three engines was lost to the men jammed in the long, shed-like building far below. It was Christmas, and for the moment the German and Austrian flyers preferred to forget the war. Through the night they had toasted the Kaiser and the Emperor Franz Josef. Other glasses had been raised to the victory of the Fatherland and the Austro-Hungarian Empire; to the Imperial German Air Force and its Austrian counterpart; to comrades living and dead. Broken glasses littered the floor and officers sprawled in deep sleep in chairs and sofas, while a small group of diehards clustered around a piano, raising their voices in song.

The party was obviously over when three uninvited guests arrived. The calling card of Bill Barker and his Canadian friends was a salvo of bombs laid neatly on the hangars, machine shops, and airplanes that were lined up along the flight line of the Austrian air base. As machine gun bullets kicked up tufts of sod all around them, mechanics vainly tried to start the cold engines of the parked planes. There was no top cover patrol, and the three Camels ranged virtually unmolested over the Austrian field, planting their bombs with deadly precision. A counter-attack in the form of heavy anti-aircraft fire was quickly organized, but the darting Sopwiths seemed to bear a charmed life. With bombs gone. they turned their guns against the planes and shops. Wingtip to wingtip, the three English planes roared across the field, so low that their wheels actually touched the ground, and poured bullets into the open doors of the hangars filled with planes. Then back into the sky they soared, machine gun belts empty. Behind them black smoke boiled into the air, and an Austrian squadron leader sadly surveyed the wreckage of what had been a crack squadron's air base.

Barker's Christmas Day attack on the enemy airfield had been unauthorized by his superiors. His spirited venture against a strongly defended installation deep inside hostile territory helped create the Barker legend but was in direct conflict with the policy of High Command. The Royal Flying Corps contingent in Italy was small, and had of necessity to conserve its men and planes. Such forays, where trained pilots and their planes were risked in assaults depending to a great extent on luck, were strictly against orders.

Although Barker and his companions kept the attack a secret, even to the point of persuading their mechanics to repair the battle damage to their planes without making a report, the Austrians and the Germans did not. German bombers attacked the field at Grossa the following day, although without much success, for several were shot down in the attack. The crew of one of the downed and captured planes were found to be wearing formal mess attire under their flying gear. When questioned, the Germans said that they had not had a chance to change from their formal uniforms in time for the raid, which was a spontaneous reaction to Barker's attack. It was only then that Wing Headquarters learned of the Christmas Day episode.

However, his superiors chose to ignore Barker's recklessness. The attack remained an open secret. Years after, flyers were still marvelling at the way those three Canadians looped their Camels disdainfully over the heads of the Austrian gunners.

This bold confrontation of the enemy, deep within his own territory, must have met with some favour at Wing Headquarters, for a week later Barker was at the head of another raiding party, this time with official sanction. The target was the Austrian Army Headquarters at Vittorio. The assignment was distant and dangerous. Number 28 Squadron provided five Camels, while a flight from another squadron and ten RE-8's made up the remainder of the force. Each plane was loaded to capacity with bombs. The attack was designed to strike a blow at the heart of the entire Austrian Army.

Through heavy anti-aircraft fire the formation reached its objective. The Camels, led by Barker, roared in to the attack. Below the level of the rooftops, they thundered down the high street of Vittorio, their guns pouring streams of lead into the windows of the large hotel which had been commandeered by the Austrian Army as its headquarters.

The slower RE-8's were just beginning to unload their bombs over the target when the first enemy fighters appeared: twelve Albatros D-5's. These were immediately engaged by the ten Camels. Then six more Austrians arrived. Ignoring the Camels, they knifed through the swirling dogfight straight for the heavily laden RE-8's. Barker was the first to see the danger that threatened the bombers and, breaking off from the main fight, he streaked after the Austrian fighters, which were closing rapidly with the British two-seaters. With his guns winking flame, Barker lunged headlong at the closest Albatros, which went over on its back and fell into a tight spin. Two more attacked him. Again, the trick he had perfected in France paid off and he whipped his plane in a tight loop. As the two heavy-nosed enemy fighters shot past, he dropped on the tail of one of them. The Austrian pilot tried desperately to avoid the stream of lead, and ran head-on into the side of a mountain. The second Albatros had had enough and steered away from the fight. The gunners of the British bombers easily beat off the now thoroughly disorganized attack of the remaining Austrian scouts.

The raids on Vittorio had been a successful beginning to the new year. By the end of January, Barker was credited with nine enemy planes destroyed, two probables, and two balloons. Since no one counted as carefully as did Barker

35

himself, the two probables on the official list could well be added to his list of confirmed victories. As the squadron record states, "... while Barker and [Captain] Mitchel [another flight leader] continued almost daily to add to their totals of decisive combats, others began to follow their lead."

The squadron was now a crack unit, composed predominantly of Canadian veterans. It was a unit that fostered a sense of pride in its members. Thus it came as a bitter blow to its top ranking ace when he was passed over for promotion to command of the squadron. Bill Barker seemed to be the logical choice to succeed Major H. F. Glanville as commanding officer when the major was transferred back to England. But it may have been Barker's very zest for action and his habit of ignoring restrictions that caused his superiors to choose another man instead. Keenly disappointed, Barker requested a transfer back to France. Instead, Wing Headquarters reassigned him to duty as a flight leader with No. 66 Squadron. Barker joined his new squadron on April 10, 1918. Despite his earlier resentment, the move was made with little bad feeling. Such transfers of senior pilots to other squadrons were commonplace, and his new wingmates welcomed the addition of such a renowned flyer to their midst.

High over the Austrian Tyrol, moonlight glinted on the wings of the huge, three-motored biplane as it banked steeply to avoid a massive mountain peak looming blue-white in the clear cold night. Below lay the darker masses of fields and forests. Muffled to the ears in his fur-lined flying suit, the pilot of the plane craned his helmeted head over the side of the cockpit and peered at the ground. Through frosted goggles, he studied the map spread out across his knees. With a gloved finger, he traced the course of a stream on the map, then compared it with the actual watercourse which gleamed silver bright in the moonlight beneath the wings of the plane.

Satisfied, the pilot's hands moved to the controls, throttling back the three motors of the giant Caproni bomber to a faint purr. Now the knife-like mountain wind seemed the sole presence in the void of space as it screamed through the maze of struts and bracing wires of the bulky airplane. Twisting in his cockpit, the pilot leaned out and pounded the fuselage with a gloved fist.

"We're here! Get ready to jump!" he shouted above the roar of the wind.

In the second cockpit of the bomber another man, similarly helmeted and clad in a flying suit, burrowed deeper behind the flimsy protection of the cockpit coaming and stared owlishly at the pilot. Aside from an involuntary clutching by gloved fingers at the bulky bundle in his lap, he gave no indication he had either heard or understood. For a brief second the plane drifted silently in the grip of the wind while the two men glared at each other. "He's not going to jump," the pilot thought angrily, "all that trouble and now he's not going to jump." His anger was understandable. He had flown the slow-moving bomber deep behind the Austrian border through skies dominated by enemy anti-aircraft guns and searchlights. It was a dangerous flight and the pilot still faced the task of returning over the same route.

The plane's passenger was also busy *with his* thoughts: "He's angry, but then, it's not his life. Who knows if this contraption will work. A parachute! I notice these flyers don't wear them. Even if it does open I'll be floating around in space like a duck in a shooting gallery." Face to face with the dangers of his first parachute jump, the spy, for that was what the passenger was, felt his determination faltering.

The mission had started an hour earlier at a British airfield along the Piave River. Accompanied by British and Italian intelligence officers, the spy, dressed as a typical Austrian businessman, had arrived at the field for his oneway plane · trip into enemy territory. He had been filled with assurances from balloon observers, who had briefed him on the intricacies of parachute jumping, that parachutes almost always worked. Now that phrase "almost always" had risen to haunt him at the moment of decision.

The pilot glanced back at his passenger once more, then, concealing a slight grin, he turned back to the controls. The plane had reached the head of the small sloping meadow that had been chosen as the drop zone. The spy's change of heart meant that they would have to make another pass over the level ground. The motors roared with full power as the pilot gently banked the big plane into a climbing turn, throttling back when the plane was again over the meadow. The passenger watched the pilot with concern. Then he settled himself more comfortably in his seat, folded his hands over the parachute and smiled. "Giving me another chance, eh? Well, I've made up my mind, Signor, I am not going to jump! You can take me back and we'll think up some other way to...." He never had a chance to complete his thought, for the pilot suddenly tripped a small lever in the cockpit and the spy's world collapsed around him. His stomach heaved as he felt himself falling through space. The bitter wind which snatched at his body was nothing to the chill of stark, physical fear that flooded every nerve. His mouth opened in a wordless scream but no sound came. Then the static line of his parachute pulled the silken canopy free, there was a sharp crack as it filled with air and a tug at shoulder and thigh as his fall was checked, and he found himself floating gently towards that hidden valley deep in the Austrian Tyrol. Anger flared as he realized that, somehow, he had been tricked by the burly Canadian flyer.

Far above, the bomber floated noiselessly down the valley, a black ghost against the stars. Bill Barker watched the tiny blossom of white drift towards the ground and nodded with satisfaction: "Mission accomplished."

Stretching his glide for as long as possible, he rode the powerful air currents of the mountains, planing the heavy aircraft like a glider, saving the engines until he was far away from the spot where he had dropped his passenger. "No use tipping them off down below," he thought.

The dark mass of the earth was looming close when he kicked the engines back into life. The twinkling lights of a village suddenly vanished and a search-light probed the darkness. "They've heard me," he muttered, shoving the stick down to gain flying speed and hammering the throttle wide open. The big plane threaded its way between the brilliant pencils of the searchlight beams. It rocked violently as blossoms of red and orange anti-aircraft bursts flared beneath its wings.

As Barker's plane laboured south, two officers stood in the shelter of a sprawling canvas hangar on a muddy flying field just behind the British trenches. The collars of their greatcoats were turned up high against the chill wind. "D'you think they made it?" The man who spoke never shifted his gaze from the blackness of the northern sky. The second man pursed his lips and remained silent. Both men turned as a sergeant of the Royal Flying Corps ran breathlessly towards them. "He's coming, sir! A forward listening post picked up the sound of his motors. He'll be here straight away."

The beat of engines overhead confirmed the sergeant's message. Officers and men poured out of the buildings at the edge of the field, and mechanics clustered in the pool of light spilling from the mouth of the hangar to stare anxiously into the darkness. Down the field, ground crewmen splashed gasoline into two shallow trenches that lined both sides of the landing strip, then tossed in burning matches. Light flared as the gasoline ignited to make a rude landing light for the plane circling in the darkness overhead. A flare popped into the sky, and a second was fired from the plane above-recognition signals. The pilots in the crowd listened carefully, gauging the distance and altitude of the descending plane. The sound suddenly changed, the engines revving. "He's down!" shouted a pilot, and the crowd surged forward.

The big Caproni waddled into the circle of light, its engines stilled, the propellers windmilling to a stop. As the men surrounded the plane, several gave low whistles as they examined the rips in the fabric of the wings and fuselage where anti-aircraft fire had scored hits. A mechanic climbed onto the wing: "Glad to see you back, sir." The pilot answered with a weary wave. He climbed stiffly from the cockpit and walked to where the two officers waited impatiently. "See you delivered our man; any trouble?" asked the taller of the two. The pilot shook his head and looked at his grinning mechanic. One eyelid dropped in a slow, meaningful wink. "We never have any trouble, do we sergeant?" he asked lightly. Eyes shining with suppressed laughter, the mechanic replied: "No sir. Not now!"

This episode was only one of many from Barker's spydropping days. Pilots rarely liked the job of delivering spies, for it posed additional hazards to those involved in combat flying. There was always the risk of a forced landing behind enemy lines due to faulty engines with the added prospect of trying to explain to the enemy the presence of the mysterious passenger, who might be wearing civilian clothes or even the uniform of a German officer. If a pilot were caught in such a situation he would invariably be executed as a spy.

Naturally, flyers were infuriated when they accepted these risks only to have the secret agent refuse to make his jump. Bill Barker solved this problem in his usual unorthodox way. With the approval of senior intelligence officers, he had a trapdoor built into the cockpit of the plane that he used for spy-dropping missions. These missions won for him one of Italy's highest military awards, the Valore Militare. The airplane added a greater mobility to the business of espionage, but Bill Barker left his personal imprint on that ancient profession.

In June, 1918, it was an open secret that the Austrian army, despite the fact that it had been shorn of its German contingents, had been regrouping for an offensive. The aim was to breach the Piave River defence line in a repeat of the victory of Caporetto, then push into the Venetian Plain and thence to central Italy. The time and place of the offensive were the only details unknown to the Allies.

British forces in Italy had been reshuffled some time earlier when some units were withdrawn to France, where they were urgently needed to repel an expected German offensive. The British now occupied trenches on the Asiago Plateau, supported by the remaining RAF units. On June 15, 1918, the Austrians began a violent bombardment along twenty-five miles of the Italo-British line. The barrage encompassed the positions of the British 23rd and 48th Divisions. A bombardment of such intensity was usually the sure sign that an attack was coming. The vital question was when? Such artillery preparation for an attack often lasted for days, which meant that front line troops were held constantly on the alert, expending nervous energy while enduring the ravages of the storm of shells. Often such defensive troops were shelled into submission long before they came to grips with enemy assault troops. It was vital to know when and where the enemy would attack so that sufficient reserves could be grouped ready to be hurled into the battle. A reconnaissance flight by Bill Barker would answer that question.

Compared with the utter desolation of France and Flanders, the face of war had been but lightly sketched on the landscape beneath the wings of Barker's Camel. The portions of ground not hidden by the smoke of bursting shells and the deadly vapour of poison gas were almost peaceful. But a closer look revealed roads jammed with men and guns, the thin tracery of trenches, and the artillery parks and d ammunition dumps.

The plane dropped lower over the battlefield as its pilot peered intently into the fog that covered the landscape. Suddenly the tiny aircraft lurched as smoke blossomed close by, and slivers of steel ripped through the air. Austrian anti-aircraft gunners had spotted the red, white, and blue roundels on the wings of Barker's plane and were sending up their greetings. More deadly black flowers dotted the sky as Barker pulled back the stick and sent his plane into a tight, climbing turn, streaking for home. He had the answer to the question that had worried the Allied High Command for days.

From the confusion below a pattern had emerged. He had noted heavy, horse-drawn wagons loaded with timbers and buttresses. Other teams of horses pulled flat-decked drays on which lay oblong objects that Barker's trained eyes had identified as pontoons. On the Austrian shoreline of the Piave River a number of these pontoons bobbed at anchor. Milling, ant-like figures were clustered around them, pushing and pulling them into a straight line that reached out into the smoky centre of the river. The river was being bridged and the concentration of floats below marked the point of the expected attack against the Allied line.

Barker's report electrified the entire Allied Command. Air units all along the front, British and Italian, went to battle stations as the word was flashed from squadron to squadron. Ground crews worked at a feverish pace to fuel and arm all available aircraft. Within hours of Barker's patrol, every plane in 14 Wing that could carry a gun or a bomb was in the air, with orders to concentrate on the Pave River bridgehead. Under the cover of a rain of shells and a blanket of gas the Austrians had already made some gains on British positions, but their key to success was the bridgehead. There was no time to group the Allied air formations for a concerted attack; they were fed into the battle piecemeal.

Despite this haphazardness, a continuous air attack was maintained against the Austrian bridging crews and the Austrian roads jammed with troops and material. By midday the weather had closed in over the battle area, but the British and Italian airmen ignored low clouds and heavy ground mist to continue their devastating assault. They salvoed their bombs into the murk, flying at zero altitude and machine-gunning every trace of the enemy troops. In the skies above the heavy cloud mass, air battles raged as Austrian fighters hammered furiously at the attacking Allied air fleet. But for once the British pilots ignored their traditional enemies in the air in favour of the more important target on the ground. The pilots knew that the embattled British forces would need all the help they could get to stem the assault of the numerically superior Austrians.

The official record of Barker's old unit, No. 28 Squadron, graphically illustrates the fury of the fight. Although darkness was rapidly approaching, a nine-plane patrol was ordered to attack the bridgehead. The patrol swept in low, bombing the boats and machine-gunning the troop formations. "Tremendous confusion resulted," the official record states. "... repair gangs were now caught unawares by the Camels and feverishly endeavoured to renew communications with the other bank [of the river]. Their efforts were not made easier by the strong currents running in the Piave. Boats were seen to sink ... and others hastily returned to the Austrian side."

Six times the Austrians bridged the river and six times these bridges were smashed by the low-flying British and Italian planes. An Austrian newsman later penned a colourful eye-witness account of the battle for his newspaper, the *Neue Freie Presse*:

> Suddenly aeroplanes also appear. They come silently down from a great height.... Now their motors hum again and their machine guns rattle. A hail of steel pelts down on the pontoons, which sink, riddled.
>
> The guns of the defence bark from the bank and fragments of their shrapnel endanger the lives of their own men, the men they wish to protect. One, two, three of the great Caproni aeroplanes descend, shot down in the mud of Montello ... like raging bulldogs, the English now advance in their furiously swift Sopwiths against our airmen, engineers, artillery and infantry.
>
> Nothing ... absolutely nothing ... avails. The enemy pilots are too numerous, the enemy's shell too many. Like Sisyphus multiplied a hundredfold, 'the bridge builders work incessantly; they fall and disappear in the flood without a cry; they launch new pontoons; they think out new methods of transport from bank to bank—nothing helps. Absolutely nothing avails. Six times are the bridges and footpaths completed, six times are they destroyed.

The despairing note of this account was well justified, for the Austrian attack was never able to get beyond its starting point. Without respite the air attack continued. Twisting and dodging over miles of enemy territory, the airmen fired their guns and dropped their bombs into dense masses of Austrian troops and equipment. Then, their ammunition exhausted, they climbed away as new flights took their place. The attack was kept up for two days. In twenty-four hours, five tons of bombs were dropped and 31,000 rounds of ammunition were expended against the Austrians by the British planes alone. The aerial attacks, combined with a series of vigorous ground attacks by British and Italian forces, not only stopped the Austrian offensive, but drove the enemy back from positions along the river which he had held for over a year.

It was the beginning of the end for the Austrian army in Italy. The entire Allied military machine had swung over to an offensive which was to become a massive drive to push the Austrians right back to the original frontier. It was only later, when their attempts to renew their offensive proved hopeless, that the Austrians realized the magnitude of their defeat on the Piave. The awesome machinery of the Allied air defences, put in motion by that solitary reconnaissance mission of Bill Barker's, had taught the Austrians one of the great new lessons of twentieth century warfare : without control of the air, ground forces are helpless.

In July, 1918, Bill Barker was promoted to the rank of major and given the command of his own squadron. Number 139 Squadron was a unit of new two-seaters : fast, heavily armed machines that were a far cry from the old slow-moving two-seaters Barker had known as a reconnaissance pilot in France.

There is no doubt that Barker would have objected to a transfer to a two-seater squadron equipped with any machine other than the new Bristol. Having made his mark as a fighter pilot, he had no intention of going back to a reconnaissance unit. However, while the Bristol was heavy enough to carry the equipment needed for aerial photography and artillery spotting, it was also a fast, highly manoeuvrable plane that could perform with the best Austrian and German fighters. Barker tried out the Bristol personally, gave it his stamp of approval, and flew the machine on many missions.

Nevertheless, he took his Camel, which now sported his personal insignia (a heart pierced with an arrow), with him when he joined 139 Squadron. His Camel was the symbol of his identity as a fighter pilot which he would never exchange for the former role of reconnaissance flyer. Tall, lean, and taciturn, Barker was still something of an enigma to his fellow flyers. A non-drinker in a job where strong liquor was often used to bolster war-shattered nerves, his very strength served to separate him from his fellows. He shunned the camaraderie of the squadron mess, preferring to spend his time on the flight line, working on his plane or guns, or dreaming up new methods of attack. Although his lengthy experience made other pilots seek his advice and counsel, his blunt manner and forceful opinions often antagonized and repelled them.

Two things in particular suited him for the command of 139 Squadron. Throughout his career, Barker had displayed a highly protective sympathy for other flyers, especially the men flying the slow-moving two-seaters. Some of his most furious attacks against enemy planes were carried out in defence of these so-called cold meat observation planes and time and again he had risked his life to save a lumbering RE-8 from the guns of enemy fighters. The high standard of performance he had previously set as an observation pilot was also in his favour. Indeed, he was the ideal choice for the command of a Brisfit unit, since the versatility of the plane demanded crews trained in both the specialized skills of observation work and the aggressive tactics of fighter pilots.

Most of the pilots of the squadron were old hands at front line flying, but none could muster the impressive record of Barker, who by this time held a Distinguished Service Order and bar, and Military Cross and bar, and had shot down thirty-three enemy aircraft and torched nine balloons. Now, with a squadron of his own, he set out to teach his men all he knew of aerial combat. His intention was obvious he planned to make 139 Squadron the most feared unit on the Italian front. To realize this goal, he led his squadron on far-ranging patrols deep into enemy territory, attacking any and all Austrian formations encountered.

In this period, following their disastrous defeat at the Piave, Austria's airmen were showing a new reticence when given the opportunity for battle. British planes were especially avoided, for the Austrian flyers by this time had a healthy respect for the hard-fighting little contingent of Royal Flying Corps aviators who had wrested control of the air from them.

In the chronicles of air combat, much has been written about the German aces who, for a time, dominated the skies of France. Less is known of the Austrian flyers *who fought* their war amidst the dangerous peaks and mountain passes of northern Italy. They were no less skilful and determined than their German cousins, but the western front in France was the main theatre of battle in the First War, and as such received more attention from the writers and historians who recorded the deeds of the early airmen. Like most pilots of the period, the majority of the aviators in the air service of the Austro-Hungarian Empire were former cavalrymen, trained for the cut and thrust tactics of an assault force. Equipped for the most part with Austrian-built prototypes of German aircraft, these former horse soldiers of the Emperor Franz Josef injected their own peculiar type of gallantry into the air fighting of the day.

One story published about Italy's leading ace, Major Francesco Baracca, demonstrates the chivalry of these onetime Austrian sabre-twirlers. Baracca was alone over the lines when he spotted a flight of fourteen Austrian planes. The formation stood between Baracca and the safety of his own territory, so, in spite of the impossible odds, the Italian attacked. Diving on the formation from behind, he shot down the last plane, dived beneath the rest, and pulled up in a tight zoom beneath the leader, downing him with another burst of machine gun fire. The astonished survivors were so impressed with the courage of this lone Italian that they formed their planes in a guard of honour around him and escorted him back to his own airfield. The story is redolent of Viennese gallantry. The manners, morals, and ideals of the nineteenth century prevailed to a great degree in the Italian campaign, which never quite reached the grey, soul-searing horror of the war in Flanders.

Barker, in his ambition to make 139 Squadron the most feared fighter unit in Italy, had made a careful study of the habits and tactics of the leading Austrian aces. Deep within his mind burned the ambition to meet and conquer each of them. He had carefully examined the careers of such notable flyers as Benno Fiala, the Ritter von Fernburgg; Godwin Brumowski, the victor of three-score aerial duels; and the foremost knight of them all, flame-haired Oberleutnant (senior lieutenant) Frank Linke-Crawford, the veteran of 150 air fights in which he had scored twentyseven victories.

The English-sounding name of Linke-Crawf ord was known and feared by Allied pilots all along the Italian front. Born of an aristocratic family in Cracow, Poland, LinkeCrawf ord was an officer in a crack Austrian cavalry regiment when the war started. He had fought gallantly on the Russian front, then, like Barker, had transferred to flying duties in 1916. He left a vivid impression on the minds of the British and Italian pilots who survived an encounter with him. Linke-Crawford's plane was distinctively decorated with a painting of the Imperial Austrian Eagle with outspread wings. He himself often flew without a helmet, his flaming red hair whipping back in the slipstream.

Day after day, Barker led his squadron over the lines, eager for a decisive encounter with any or all of the top Austrian squadrons, or Fliks. Although there was plenty of action for the eager pilots of 139 Squadron, the champions of Austria were either on the ground or somewhere else when battle was joined.

Barker decided that the time had come for a direct approach, and the course he adopted was that of issuing a blanket challenge to all the Austrian aces. The challenge, written in German and printed on thousands of leaflets, was couched in terms of subtle insult designed to enrage the haughty Austrians : "Major W. G. Barker, DSO, Mc, and the officers under his command, present their compliments to Captains Brumowski, Ritter von Fiala, Havratil and the pilots under their command [this included the redoubtable Linke-Crawford] and request the pleasure of a meeting in the air. In order to save Captains Brumowski, Ritter von Fiala and Havratil and the gentlemen of their party the inconvenience of searching for them, Major Barker and his officers will bomb Godega Aerodrome at 10 a.m. daily, weather permitting, for the next fortnight."

These leaflets were dropped by the thousands over the Austrian lines by Barker's planes. The Austrian pilots were properly angered, but they were not given the chance to accept the challenge. Their superiors were alert to the danger of such a meeting and the possibility that the encounter would cost them some of their best men, to no tactical advantage. So despite the humiliation, the high-born flyers of Austria were ordered to stay clear of all such duels with Barker and his "wild Canadians." In the meantime, Barker cooly fulfilled his promise and bombed Godega airfield daily, "weather permitting."

Despite the suggestion of timidity, there is no doubt that the decision of the Austrian Command was the right one. The duel proposed by Barker would have fitted perfectly the assignment of the British air units in Italy—the destruction of Austrian air power. The Allies might thus have won undisputed control of the air, and the airmen had already demonstrated at the Piave crossing their ability to be a decisive factor in the progress of the war. Austrian power both in the air and on the ground-was on the wane, and the Austrians could ill afford to lose their remaining strength in an aerial tournament.

There was one strong reaction, however, to Barker's impudent challenge. In retaliation for the bombing attacks on Godega, the Austrians appealed to the Germans for help, and a force of long-range Gotha bombers was sent to Italy. Barker met this threat as he met every challenge. Alerted that the bombers were heading for his field, Barker ordered every plane into the air to meet them. He was the first to lift his wheels from the landing strip and had gained considerable altitude before he met the German formation. The bulky Gothas were considered dangerous opponents, for by maintaining tight formation they could bring considerable firepower to bear on attacking fighters. Barker met them head on, flying straight down the flight path of the leading bomber, his guns flaming. The heavy twin-engine bomber slipped off on one wing and Barker dived beneath the formation, zooming up to "hang on his prop" in a near stall as he poured another deadly volley into the belly of the last bomber in the formation as it passed overhead. This one too went into a dive and crashed far below. The German formation lost heavily to Barker's men and the attack was a failure.

In this flight Barker again managed to introduce something new in tactics. He attacked from the head-on position. This way, only the nose guns of the bombers could be brought to bear on his charging aircraft. He would roar in to the attack, his plane upside down, then dive away at the last minute only to pull up in a steep zoom that would again bring him to the front of the formation. Years later, in 1943 and 1944, the nose gunners of RAF and USAF bombers attacking Germany marvelled at the daring German fighters who roared head-on into the bomber formations, rolling on their backs while they sprayed the oncoming bombers with bullets, then plummeting away in an inverted dive before all the defensive guns could be brought into action. These German pilots were, perhaps unwittingly, paying tribute to Barker's sense of tactics. In Italy, even the most cautious knew the Allied victory was at hand. On the ground the Austrian army was in full retreat, and in the air the Austrians avoided action unless it was forced on them.

The attention of the world was now given fully to France, where a furious battle had broken out along the western front. For months the Germans had husbanded their strength for an all-out attempt to break the Allied line and push through to Paris and victory. The first of a series of offensives to achieve this end had been launched in March, 1918, when German attacks smashed against the British Third and Fifth Armies. In less than two weeks the Germans had pushed the British lines back forty miles. Then Generals Ludendorff and Hindenburg, the joint commanders of the German Army, launched another assault against the French in Champagne. Germany had bolstered its western forces with forty-two divisions drawn from the Russian front, with the aim of achieving a decisive victory before fresh American troops arrived. The reinforced German army smashed against disorganized French troops still recovering from wholesale mutinies and against a British force weakened by heavy losses in Flanders.

German attacks were renewed in July and it was during this critical period that the Allied airmen put the value of air power beyond question. They were called on to fill the gaps in the Allied defence created by losses on the ground. Airplanes had become flying pillboxes and machine gun nests. Almost every squadron on the front was ordered into the counter-attack against the Germans and, just as in the fighting at the Piave River, the airplanes fought desperately to halt the German advance.

With such fierce fighting raging in France, Major Bill Barker became restless. Galled by the inactivity of Italy now that victory was near, he applied for a transfer

Undated photo shows a Sopwith 7F.1 Snipe scout fighter. Designed to succeed the Camel, it had greater power --
the 230-hp Bentley Rotary B.R. 2 engine -- a similarly tight turning circle and excellent rate of climb, but none
of its forebear's unforgiving nature. It carried one pilot, two Vickers .303-in. machine guns in a Camel-like fairing
and four 25-lb. bombs on underfuselage racks. Deliveries began in the summer of 1918 and about 200 were delivered
before the Armistice. Canada's Maj. W.G. Barker won the Victoria Cross for an Oct. 27, 1918, battle in which he
single-handedly took on 15 Fokker D.VIIs. In all, 497 Snipes were built and the type remained in RAF service
until 1926.
Department of National Defence/M-952

to the more vital theatre of war. When his orders finally arrived in September,
1918, it came as a shock to learn he had been transferred to Hounslow, England,
to take command of another flying school.

His first impulse was to refuse point blank. His second was to use diplomacy.
On his arrival at Hounslow, it was a new Barker who affably agreed that only a
veteran of many air battles could properly teach the secrets of manoeuvre and
gunnery to the fledgling airmen of the school. However, he added, how could a
man instruct these youngsters if he himself was not fully abreast of all the latest
trends in air combat tactics and the latest equipment now in use? Patiently he
explained that the enemy aircraft encountered in Italy were generally older and
less efficient than the new Fokker *D-7's now in use* in France. Also, he added,
tactics in France differed greatly. The sixty-plane flying circuses of German
aircraft now regularly patrolling the western front had no counterpart in Italy,
where the scope of air fighting was restricted to small formations. How could
a man explain tactics on the basis of out-dated experience?

The argument seemed reasonable enough to the senior officers at Headquarters
(who, no doubt, were relieved to find Barker such an agreeable man after the tales

they had heard). So they gave Barker his wish—a roving commission to operate along the western front, moving from sector to sector to wherever the fighting was thickest. With the assignment went a brand new fighter plane—the Sopwith Snipe, the latest of a distinguished line of fighter aircraft turned out by the Sopwith factory.

The Snipe was designed as the successor to the Camel, and it resembled the older fighter in many ways. It went into production only three months before the war ended, and, consequently, only a few saw actual service at the front. Powered by a 230-horsepower Bentley rotary engine, which produced a speed of 113 miles an hour at 15,000 feet, the Snipe had all the advantages of the Camel and none of its drawbacks. It carried twin Vickers guns under an enclosure similar to the famous "hump" which had earned the Camel its name. It was with high hopes that Barker took this efficient little fighter into action.

For several weeks he roamed the battle zones, choosing the hottest sectors in which to bed down with the line squadrons. Since there were fewer than one hundred Snipes in action in France at the time, his plane was a curiosity to the members of the squadrons he visited. Needless to say, Barker had ample opportunity to demonstrate the aircraft's ability in the furious air fighting that raged along the entire front during this period.

It was clear that the war was moving swiftly to an end. The German Army had virtually committed suicide in its final bid for victory. It had lost close to 700,000 men, many of them the finest troops of the Fatherland, in the three months of attack on the Allied positions. When these offensives had finally ground to a halt, the initiative passed to the Allies. Field Marshal Foch of France, the Commander-in-Chief of all Allied armies, was not slow to grasp his opportunity. With 100,000 fresh American troops spearheading masses of tanks, he launched vigorous counter-attacks which developed into a great offensive.

The British commander, Field Marshal Haig, was also on the move in Flanders. His armies broke through the German defences and hordes of cavalry were loosed in the German rear. (The cavalry forces had waited almost four years for this opportunity.) But Germany's impending defeat was not apparent in the air. German squadrons were now equipped with the latest products of the fertile brain of aircraft designer Anthony Fokker, the D-7 and D-8, high performance fighters that were exacting a stiff toll from Allied flyers.

Barker's victory tally now totalled forty-seven, which placed him fourth in the roster of Canadian aces, with fellow Canadian Billy Bishop's seventy-two victories unequalled by any other living flyer. That was the standing on the morning of October 27, 1918, when Bill Barker packed his personal belongings and prepared to return to England. He had been staying with No. 201 Squadron, a Camel unit with a large number of Canadians in it, when orders had come through for him to return.

Higher authorities now felt that he had had plenty of time to acquire the first-hand information necessary to teach young pilots the tricks of air fighting. Barker's life was now considered too valuable to risk in the daily dogfights over the western front. The order had been final, and Barker realized that this time there was no chance of arguing his way out of it. So with his baggage packed and ready for ground transport to England, he walked to his plane, carrying only a small kit bag for the return flight across the Channel. Mechanics had been busy that morning stripping the Snipe of its war loading in preparation for the more peaceful life of a training station. Though the guns were loaded, the Aldis peep sight had been removed and only the open ring sight left in place.

Barker climbed into the cockpit and waved away the mechanics. The plane roared down the field; then it seemed to head off in the wrong direction. An hour later, phones jangled in the squadron's operations office and breathless front line artillery observers related to the thunderstruck aviators of 201 Squadron the garbled details of one of the most astounding air battles in aviation history.

Barker had indeed flown in the wrong direction. He had purposely set his course for the battlefront. Later he admitted that he wanted "one last look," and possibly one last tangle with German fighters before calling it quits.

After take-off he held the nose of the Snipe in a steady climb, the little aircraft responding beautifully to his touch on the controls. At 15,000 feet, he levelled off and flew, parallel to the front lines. The town of Cambrai was behind him when he swung the plane into a half turn and held his course steady into German-dominated air space. Climbing again, he brought the labouring Snipe up to 19,000 feet. This was almost the ceiling for the plane, and Barker found himself breathing quickly in the thin air. Then, far ahead, he spotted puffs of smoke from bursting anti-aircraft shells high in the sky over the Allied section of the front line. That spelled out a warning: enemy aircraft. Barker dipped one wing and banked away towards the anti-aircraft fire. Black crosses glinted in the sunlight and Barker made out the silhouette of a high-flying German observation plane. German two-seaters of 1918 were particularly efficient in the thin air of extreme altitudes, and there were few British machines that could catch them. Nevertheless, the Snipe, with part of its war loading stripped away, responded when Barker again eased the stick back, and rose above its ceiling of 20,000 feet.

Reports vary about the type of aircraft Barker was stalking, but it was probably either a late model Rumpler or the formidable Hanoveranner, an armour-plated machine that was among the best fighter aircraft. Both these aircraft were deadly foes. The Rumpler, described as one of the finest two-seaters of the war, could reach 21,000 feet and carried three machine guns. An earlier model of the Rumpler was credited with shooting down the famous French ace, Georges Guynemer.

Besides their own defensive armament, two-seaters on reconnaissance missions rarely travelled alone. There were invariably a number of "little friends" hovering in the sun, ready to pounce on any Allied plane that came too close. Barker was fully aware of his danger as he nursed his labouring plane into a position for attack. He searched the sky for signs of enemy fighters, but found none. By this time he was on a level with the two-seater and the enemy pilot had evidently spotted him, for the German plane turned eastward towards home. Barker dipped the nose of his plane slightly to gain flying speed and the chase was on. The two planes were now heading at top speed directly into German-held territory. The risk to Barker increased with every mile, for at any moment a German formation could come between him and his own lines, cutting off his chance of retreat.

The German plane was flying straight and level in a bid to outrun the faster Snipe. Despite the fact that his controls were now mushy owing to the height, Barker sacrificed some of his speed to gain a few more precious feet of altitude, then lunged at the two-seater. The German manoeuvred violently to give the gunner a clear field of fire, turning first to the left, then to the right. Barker nosed down until he was below the enemy's tail, then pulled his Snipe into a gentle climb, hoping to reach the blind spot beneath the tail where he could rake the other ship with his fire without danger.

But this German proved to be wily. While the pilot yawed the plane violently, the observer swung his gun over the side and bullets thudded into Barker's plane. It was a point-blank shot at the slowly climbing Snipe and every bullet struck home with telling effect. Barker pulled away from the damaging fire and circled the two-seater warily. His plan of attack had been foiled by the Germans' expert handling of their equipment. He realized then that his only course was to try and out-shoot the observer. Again he approached from the rear, but this time at an angle, hoping to make a deflection shot which would knock out the enemy plane before the observer's fire could be brought to bear on him. Again bullets beat a tattoo against the thin fabric of the Snipe, but Barker grimly held his course. At forty yards, the enemy plane was centred in his ring sight and he thumbed the firing button on his control stick. A stream of Vickers bullets stitched a line of holes across the fuselage of the two-seater.

Barker watched as his enemy plunged towards the earth far below, a greasy plume of smoke marking its fall. It was victory number forty-eight for the Canadian. Groggy from the lack of oxygen and the excitement of the fight, he felt a mild surprise as parachutes blossomed behind. the burning aircraft; it was the first time that Barker had seen parachutes used by a plane crew.

There was no time to marvel at the new development. A vicious blow struck him in the right thigh, and bullets hammered his instrument panel to junk. In sudden panic he looked behind him straight into the winking muzzles of two Spandau machine guns. A German fighter had arrived too late to help the two-seater and was now out for vengeance. The bullet which struck Barker was an explosive round, and it had shattered his leg. Almost fainting with pain, he lost control of the Snipe, which fell off into a flat spin. The enemy fighter followed him down, evidently satisfied that the British plane or its pilot was disabled. After a 2,000-foot plunge, Barker managed to regain control, and, pulling the stick back to his safety-belt, he turned to face his attacker. With his first burst he torched the enemy plane.

This was not the end, though. Faint from pain, Barker had set his course for the British lines when tracers again whispered past his cockpit. He looked above him : the sky was filled with black-crossed airplanes. His plane had passed right through a formation of at least twenty of the lethal new Fokker D-7's. It was sheer instinct that guided Barker's hand as he pulled the stick back, at the same time tramping hard with his good leg on the rudder bar. The Snipe spun around and Barker bored in towards the closest Fokker, his guns hammering. His glazed eyes, peering through the ring sight, soon told him that he was actually attacking two planes, one right behind the other. With a ferocity born of desperation, Barker continued his charge and was rewarded by seeing both Fokkers, their wings riddled with bullets, fall off into power spins. Meanwhile a third German fighter loomed in his sights. At ten yards Barker's bullets struck home and the German plane exploded. Then Barker was hit again; this time the bullet broke the bone in his left leg. The world turned grey, then black, as he lost consciousness. Again the Snipe fell off into a spin. The rush of air revived him and instinctively he levelled off, right in the centre of another German formation.

The bullet-torn Snipe had fallen below 15,000 feet now and the beleaguered Canadian fell back on the one manoeuvre that could save him. He put the Snipe into a tight turn and as he circled he fired at everything that crossed his path. With a German right behind him, he tacked himself on the tail of another brightly coloured Fokker, watching with dazed satisfaction as his bullets went home and a trickle of flame, followed by a fiery gust of smoke, burst from the

Fokker's motor. Again he felt the shock of a bullet and his left arm went limp—an explosive bullet had broken his elbow. Once more he fainted and his plane fell into a spin. His pursuer drew off, certain that he had finally downed this apparently indestructible Canadian.

However, at 12,000 feet the higher oxygen content of the air revived Barker, and once more he pulled up his battered plane just in time. But the nightmare continued: Barker found himself in the midst of a third echelon of German planes. Contemporaries believe that Barker must have tangled with an entire flying circus stepped up in flights, or *Jagdestaffeln* (hunting squadrons), of twenty planes each. As he lost altitude in his uncontrolled spins his plane passed successively from one flight to another. Ground observers later swore they counted as many as sixty planes lining up in "taxi-rank" for a shot at this madman who did not know when he was beaten. Barker said later he was certain that he was doomed and had resolved to sell his life as dearly as possible.

Now, in the midst of the lowest level of the German circus, the severely wounded Canadian aimed his plane at the nearest Fokker. Barker wanted to ram this German before he died. He poured bullets at the German plane as he roared towards it, and watched in dazed disbelief as it disintegrated in mid-air, so that he literally flew right through the wreckage of the enemy plane.

Again the infuriated Germans closed in and Barker's plane shuddered under a fresh onslaught of bullets. Tracers tore into the gas tank of the Snipe, but luck was still with him, for his plane did not catch fire. Switching to his auxiliary tank, he kept the tattered Snipe in the air by sheer force of will. No man's land was skimming beneath his wheels; ahead lay the British trenches and safety. Barker fought back the black tide of unconsciousness and, with his remaining strength, hauled the control stick back into his stomach. The Snipe lifted slightly, soaring over the tangles of barbed wire that marked the British front line, then settled wearily to earth. The wheels snubbed into a shell hole and the plane nosed over.

Scottish troops who pulled Barker's unconscious body from the wreckage had watched most of the fight from their trenches. They had seen Barker's suicidal lunge at the last Fokker and his intention had been obvious. They were astounded to find the badly shot-up airman still alive. Barker was in a coma for two weeks and only his amazing vitality saved his life. His wounds left him with permanent and painful disabilities. When he regained consciousness, he learned that the war was over and he had won the Victoria Cross-the third Canadian flyer to receive the Empire's highest award in the First World War. Barker's epic battle remains a classic in the annals of aerial warfare. It brought him promotion from the rank of major to lieutenant-colonel. He was given credit for the destruction of five German aircraft in the battle, which brought his final tally up to fifty-two aircraft and nine balloons destroyed, the sixth highest total in the entire RAF.

The true measure of Barker's courage is illustrated by his attitude to life after the war. The wounds he had received refused to heal properly and he was in constant torment. Yet walking only with the help of canes, he continued to lead the active life of a flyer. He helped to found the Royal Canadian Air Force and, with the great Billy Bishop, started Canada's first airline. There are no medals for this kind of courage. Barker's refusal to surrender to his crippling injuries reveals his unconquerable spirit more than all his deeds in battle. Ironically, in March, 1930, while making a routine test flight of a new plane at Uplands Airport, Ottawa, the man who had survived the most one-sided fight in aviation history crashed to his death.

Four Canadians Named "Mac"

In 1917, the various roles of aircraft in aerial combat had not been clearly defined. Sometimes fighters actually carried out jobs that today would be assigned to bombers. Likewise, bombers were often called on to engage enemy planes, the traditional role of the fighter. This overlapping of roles is illustrated by the careers of four young Canadians whose names began with "Mac," and who performed their varied duties with a daring that won for them the highest awards their country could bestow.

Don MacLaren was born in Ottawa, but grew up at an Indian trading post in the remote Peace River country of British Columbia. There he mastered the Cree tongue and, in his many encounters with the wilderness, developed a hardy sense of independence. There, too, his father gave him the training in the use of firearms which, a few years later, was to make Don MacLaren one of the deadliest flying machine-gunners on the western front.

The war seemed far away from Peace River until, one day in 1916, Don MacLaren returned from a government survey into the far north to learn that his older brother had enlisted in the Canadian Army. MacLaren made his decision at once. Instead of the Army, he elected to join the Royal Flying Corps. He was sent to Camp Borden to take flight training and in the autumn of 1917 he received his wings. The graduation was something of a milestone, for he was among the first pilot-trainees to complete their entire training in Canada.

On his arrival in France in November, 1917, Don MacLaren was attached to No. 46 Squadron on the Arras-Cambrai front. At that time he had no opportunity to display the ability that would distinguish him as an aerial duellist, for Germany was conserving its air power for a large-scale attack. The Sopwith Camels of 46 Squadron, finding few enemy planes on their patrols over the lines, confined themselves to tactical ground support missions. It was not until late February of 1918 that MacLaren scored his first victory, over a German Pfalz. From then on his score rose rapidly as plane after plane fell before his guns. In March, 1918, MacLaren's career reached its peak.

That spring, the lull on the Arras-Cambrai front had been broken by a series of strong German attacks against the British lines. The attacks were supported

by the destructive power of a number of huge railroad guns that were systemati-
cally smashing British communication lines, railheads, and ammunition dumps.
These guns were huge, sixteen-inch naval rifles. Too large for conventional gun
carriages, they were mounted on railroad flatcars and could be moved at will over
railways behind the German front to any part of the line where they were needed.
From camouflaged rail sidings, the guns could pour a salvo of shells into British
emplacements and then move to another location before counter-battery fire
could be brought to bear on them. The guns were located six miles behind the
German front, ringed with anti-aircraft batteries, and protected by a heavy screen
of fighters. To attack them from the air would require planes capable of battling
their way into, and out of, the target. This meant fighters, and MacLaren's
squadron was assigned the job of destroying one of the big rifles, located at a
rail siding at Brebieres.

Eight Camels, fully loaded with twenty-pound Cooper bombs, were sent out
from the squadron to do the job. The pilots in the formation were fully aware
of the perils of their mission. Even though they were flying fighter planes, their
machines were so heavily laden with bombs that they would be fair game for any
high-flying enemy fighter. Moreover, while over the target they would have to

1918 photo shows a Sopwith F.1 Camel, flown by Lt. William S. Lockhart, outside a hangar at Turnhouse,
Scotland. It was distinguished by its snub nose, the pronounced dihedral of its bottom wing and the "hump" --
covering the breeches of its twin Vickers machine guns atop the fuselage -- that gave what was first called the
Sopwith Biplane F.1 its name. Though tricky to master, it was virtually unrivalled in its manoeuvrability.
Equipped with a 130-hp Clerget rotary engine -- one of several Camel powerplants -- it had top speed of 115 mph
at 6,500 feet and service ceiling of 19,000 feet. The camel was 18 ft. 9 in. long, spanned 28 ft., stood 8 ft. 6 in.
high and weighed a maximum 1,453 lb. on takeoff. 5,490 Camels were built.
Department of National Defence/DND65-90

57

fly very in order to place their bombs accurately, and they therefore be within range of even the smallest anti-air weapons. As the formation approached the target, the planes strung out in single file to make their pass over the huge gun. Tracer bullets filled the air around them as they roared dove the camouflaged emplacement. Geysers of smoke and rose from detonating bombs, but the huge cannon appeared to be indestructible. Then came MacLaren's turn. Diving so low that he could hardly miss, he tripped the bomb release at the last possible moment, scoring two direct on the gun and two more on the railway tracks. His plane was so low that it rocked with the concussion of its own bomb bursts.

Their mission accomplished, the British planes had grouped for the flight home when MacLaren suddenly spotted a German two-seater below him. He dived after it and a burst of one hundred rounds sent the German spinning into the ground near the outskirts of Douai. Looking upwards to search the sky for his companions, MacLaren realized that he was now alone. By this time German A-A guns had found his range and shells were bursting all around his plane. Hedgehopping to avoid the fire, he almost ran head-on into a German observation balloon. Banking in a steep turn, MacLaren sent a volley of fire into the bag, which exploded into flame.

The young Canadian was doing so well that he decided not to go home just then. Flying circuits over the area, he was suddenly attacked from above by a brilliant green two-seater, which dived beneath the Camel and zoomed straight up, raking MacLaren's machine with fire from both its forward and after guns. MacLaren half-rolled away from the plane, a Hanoveranner, and the two aircraft cautiously circled each other, searching for an opening. The tighter turn of the Camel prevailed. MacLaren found himself inside the turning radius of the other plane and his hammered a long burst, stitching the German plane from propeller to tail. It nosed over in a steep dive and crashed near Marquion. Having removed the last immediate threat to his presence, MacLaren headed home. For this brilliant diaplay of daring and skill he received the Military Cross.

Don MacLaren was one of the lucky ones who survived var. With fifty-four kills, he emerged as the RAF's fifth-ranking ace and Canada's third-ranking one. He held also Distinguished Service Order, the Military Cross and bar, the Croix de guerre, and the ribbon of the French Légion d'honneur. In peacetime he followed a career in civil aviation, serving as an executive with Trans-Canada Airlines. When war began again, in 1939, this versatile and distinguished airman served his country once more as a senior officer in the RCAF.

One of the strangest careers of the First World War was that of Captain G.E.H. McElroy. Born in Windsor, Ontario, according to some records, or Dublin,

Ireland, according to others, he was apparently the son of an Irish schoolmaster. What is certain is that he grew up in Canada, and war records state that during the first months of the war he served as a dispatch rider with an artillery unit in England. However, his desire to be in the thick of the fighting prompted to apply for a transfer to the Royal Flying Corps. In February, 1916, his wish was granted, and he was accepted for flight training.

McElroy arrived at the training school only to encounter problems. It was obvious from the start that he was far from a born flyer. Willing, but hopelessly clumsy, he was injured several times in crash landings. Class after class graduated and received their wings, and McElroy was still using circuits and bumps over the field. His superiors began to despair of ever seeing him leave. At last he mast his lessons sufficiently well to graduate, but even then he was not considered good front line material and was kept in England on home defence patrols. Finally, in August, 1917, he was transferred to France and attached to No. 40 Squadron, stationed at Bruay.

The squadron was equipped with the Nieuport, a light-weight, French-made fighter powered by a rotary engine. The Nieuport was a duellist's weapon, responding instantly, like a rapier, to the slightest touch on the controls. Because of the plane's sensitivity, disaster once more came close ending McElroy's flying career. The Canadian's ham-fisted approach to flying was too much for the French plane, and he crashed two of them in one day, narrowly escaping injury.

Before his despairing squadron commander could send him back to England, however, McElroy's luck changed. The squadron was re-equipped with a new SE-5 fighter, a sturdier aircraft, better suited than the Nieuport to McElroy's flying style. Piloting the SE-5 during the last few days of 1917, he shot down three German planes, two of them in the same fight. From that point on, McElroy's name figured more and more often in combat dispatches from the front.

Once he had acquired complete confidence, McElroy was a vicious aerial executioner with an unquenchable thirst for victims. He waged indiscriminate war on any plane with black crosses on its wings. Many pilots regarded the enemy—both in the air and on the ground—with a philosophical respect and tolerance. Not so McElroy. For some reason he hated Germans. He drove himself with a punishing fury that left him physically and mentally exhausted, and almost alienated his comrades. In aerial combat he attacked with what seemed to be blind rage, taking no stock of the numbers or strength of his opponents. His battle reports indicate the aggressiveness of his tactics. On January 16, 1918, when he downed two DFW two-seater observation planes, he ignored a heavy escort of six Pfalz Scouts to press home the attack, shooting down one of the single-seaters in the process. O March 9, he attacked a formation of nine Fokker Triplanes, shooting one down and chasing the remainder all the way back to their aerodrome. Again, that same day, he attacked a German Halberstadt two-seater that was strafing a British advance post and, with a single burst, sent it spinning into he ground.

In earlier days, two-seaters had been considered easy targets for fighter pilots, but at this stage of the war they were among the finest performers in the air. It was in dealing with two-seaters that McElroy was particularly ruthless. The heavily armoured Halberstadts, with their deadly ability for contour flying, and the fast, manoeuvrable Rumplers were his most bitter foes. Like most pilots, McElroy had served with the infantry and he felt a deep bond of sympathy for the heavily burdened ground troops enduring the grey horror of the trenches. It was a matter of conscience for him to offer himself as their aerial champion, protecting them from the bombardments and machine gun attacks of the German two-seater observation and ground attack planes. In defence of British ground troops under air attack he would fly like a madman. Unlike some pilots, who shunned ground-strafing missions because of the deadly anti-aircraft fire they had to face, he flew his plane recklessly through hurricanes of bullets to knock out German machine gun nests and artillery batteries. During the British retreat of March, 1918, he flew an average of five sorties a day to help retreating Allied troops escape the advancing Germans.

Such a pace took its toll. By April McElroy was exhausted and ill. With thirty-eight confirmed victories to his credit he was sent to England on leave. Early in the summer of 1918, however, he was back in action. Now a captain and holder of the Military Cross, he was reassigned to No. 40 Squadron.

By the time McElroy arrived the Germans were again reasserting themselves. Germany had designed new fighter planes which had once again given them a slight edge over the Allies. One of these was the deadly Fokker D-7, a blunt-nosed fighter that "climbed like an elevator" and had the ability to hang on its prop and shoot the floorboards out of planes passing above it. But apparently the new enemy fighter held no terrors for McElroy. In less than two months he added twelve more victories to his total, most of them D-7's.

At this time, he narrowly escaped death when his plane suddenly caught fire during a fight with a two-seater. The British lines were not far away and McElroy tipped his plane up on one wing and sideslipped it to the ground. He landed safely, escaping with minor burns.

Eleven days later, on July 31, time ran out for the Canadian flyer. He had taken off for a solo patrol after his usual careful inspection of his plane and guns.

It was a misty day, and McElroy's plane was soon lost to the sight of the men at the field. Hours passed and he did not return. Anxious telephone messages went out from the squadron's headquarters to front line observation posts in an attempt to learn his fate, but no one had seen an SE-5 crash anywhere along the front. German intelligence reports made no reference to the destruction of McElroy's plane and his fate remains as mysterious today as his personal background. His aircraft could have vanished into a cloud during to be destroyed by the heavy artillery fire that raged along the front; or perhaps his ferocity in tracking down his prey led him across the German lines to be massacred by uneven odds.

We shall never know exactly the origins of McElroy's ferocity in battle. It may have been prompted by self-doubt. His early failures as a pilot indicate that he had none of the flair for flying that distinguished other leading aces. When he finally did find the secret through hard work, courage, and determination, he may have feared that any let-up in the gruelling pace he set himself would lose him the magic of his success. His apparent oblivion to danger, and his hatred of the enemy, would seem to have been rooted in more than simple patriotic ardour. Probably McElroy hated the Germans because he feared them and nursed a terror that one day he would react too late and find himself a victim to the guns of a German fighter. The dreaded moment may finally have come that day when McElroy disappeared.

Alan McLeod had no business being an ace. No one expected him to shoot down enemy aircraft. His job was observation and bombardment. The plane he flew, an Armstrong-Whitworth, was generally only used for these two jobs because of its slow flying speed and stability in the air. Indeed, the old Ack-W had the stability of a freight train and was about as easy to handle. Yet with the help of his observer, McLeod knocked down the required number of enemy aircraft to earn the title of "ace." In time, he was to become Canada's second aviator to win the Victoria Cross.

McLeod was born in 1899, the son of a country doctor in a little Manitoba town called Stonewall. Army life appealed to him early in his life, and at fourteen, concealing his age, he enlisted with the Fort Garry Horse militia regiment as a summer soldier. When the war started, the year its enlistment, his age was discovered, and, despite his repeated entreaties, his application for overseas service was refused. It was not until the spring of 1917, at the eighteen, that McLeod managed to be accepted as a cadet in the RFC. He proved to be a natural pilot and soloed after only three sessions of dual control instruction. But even with his wings, McLeod's youth was still against him. Instead of the front line duty he wanted, he was assigned to a home defence squadron in England. Only in November, 1917,

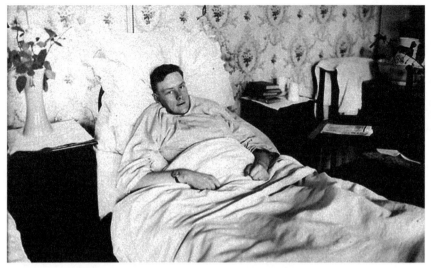

Lt. Alan Arnett McLeod, V.C.
Canada Dept. of National Defence/National Archives of Canada/PA-006736

at the ripe age of nineteen, was he transferred at last to No. 2 Squadron in France.

While McLeod would have preferred a fighter group, he carried out the dull but dangerous observation work allotted to 2 Squadron with such skill that he soon gained the admiration of the veteran pilots. To satisfy his yearning for action he spiced up his assignments with dangerous forays into territory dominated by German fighters. Although the poor speed of his plane was against him, the records show that he was a dangerous adversary.

One day, while McLeod was on his way home from a mission, three vari-coloured German fighters slipped out of a cloudbank and pounced on his lumbering Armstrong-Whitworth. While his observer peppered the pursuing fighters with volleys from his Lewis gun, McLeod quickly shoved the plane's nose down to gain flying speed and headed for the British lines. Dodging violently, the plane passed over no man's land. Ahead lay the comparative safety of the British front lines. The German pilots were reforming for a final attempt to down the slow-moving Ack-W when they got the surprise of their lives.

Noting that his pursuers were badly strung out, McLeod seized the opportunity to exploit their carelessness. Banking around in a tight turn, he roared back at the nearest fighter, closing rapidly with it until the brightly coloured German plane filled the ring sight of his machine gun. McLeod thumbed the firing button. A stream of lead smashed in the craft and it fell into a flat spin.

The shock effect of this manoeuvre on the remaining Germans gave McLeod the time to make his escape.

McLeod's squadron mates were just as surprised as the Germans when McLeod's observer told them excitedly the victory. It was not often that an Armstrong Whitworth emerged victorious in a struggle with the fast German fighters. Just a month later the youthful pilot attempted an equally impossible task when he attacked a German observation balloon near Lille. Observation balloons were always heavily protected by fighters and anti-aircraft guns, and only the fastest fighters were assigned to destroy they. Despite this, McLeod, with his youthful enthusiasm convinced his observer, Roger Keys, that it was worth trying.

Moving slowly through the hail of anti-aircraft fire McLeod bore relentlessly in on the balloon. At point-blank range, he opened fire. To his elation the balloon burst into flame. Then, as McLeod was pulling his plane into a climbing turn, three Albatross fighters dropped on his tail. It was a repetition of the earlier flight, with the young Canadian weaving his plane to avoid the tracers of the pursuing Germans as he laboured towards the safety of the British lines. This time it was the observer who scored the hit. Roger Keys poured a full drum of ammunition into the motor of the nearest German, who shot towards the ground, while the remaining two pulled up short and circled away. McLeod's Armstrong-Whitworth was becoming as deadly as a fighter.

When the German offensive of March, 1918, began, McLeod's unit was pressed into the same ground-support role that was assigned McElroy's squadron. For days on end every British plane that could carry a gun or a bomb was sent out to attack the German shock troops, artillery batteries, and rail centres. On the morning of March 27, McLeod's plane was loaded with bombs for an attack against a German battery in the Bray-sur-Somme region. It was the third such mission that he had carried out in twelve hours, and both McLeod and his observer were suffering from a lack of proper sleep and food. With five other planes, McLeod's machine lifted from the field and vanished in the heavy fog that shrouded the area—the same fog that had helped the Germans mount a surprise attack against the British lines. The weather thickened further as the formation approached the front and McLeod, flying only by compass, soon found himself separated from his companions. With his gasoline running low, and still unable to locate his target after two dangerously low descents, he swung back to British territory and landed at another British flying field to get his bearings. Heavily laden with bombs, the plane landed badly and the under-carriage was damaged. McLeod and his new observer, Lieutenant A.H. Hammond, stayed for lunch with the commanding officer while mechanics made repairs. (Hammond had replaced Keys as McLeod's observer several weeks earlier. An experienced gunner, who already held the Military Cross, Hammond was a kindred spirit for the adventure-seeking young Canadian. As a team, they had won permission from their commanding officer to carry out a variety of missions that were far removed from the regular assignments of the squadron.)

When the damage to their plane had been mended and the fog had cleared somewhat, the pair took off once more. McLeod was still trying to find the target through the heavy ground mists when a deadly Fokker Triplane appeared suddenly, boring in on a collision course. Instantly McLeod pressed the trigger of his machine gun and tracers lanced through the mist at the oncoming German plane. The triplane zoomed over the top wing of the two-seater and Hammond raked the passing plane with several volleys from his Lewis gun. The German fighter went over on its back into an out-of-control spin.

The German had not been alone, though. High overhead, seven more of the brightly coloured triplanes, members of the feared von Richthofen circus, tilted into a dive and roared down on the British plane from every direction. Bullets pounded McLeod's aircraft, damaging the controls and simultaneously wounding both pilot and observer. Coolly, McLeod manoeuvred to give Hammond the chance to bring his gun to bear on the German fighters. With short bursts, the observer tried to drive off the attackers, and his aim was good, for another triplane suddenly tipped down and spun for the earth. The infuriated survivors closed in again, and one, zooming under the two-seater, pounded it with a long burst of fire at point-blank range. One of the bullets found its mark and once more McLeod was wounded, while another tracer slug pierced the fuel tank, sending flames bursting from the motor. The exultant triplanes moved in for the kill—only to be met with a burst of bullets from Hammond's rear gun. McLeod, meanwhile, had put the plane into an easy glide and wiggled out of the cockpit, climbing warily onto the lower wing. From this precarious perch, with only his flying suit and gloves to protect him from the searing flames, he worked the controls, dropping the left wing so that the plane went into a sideslip which blew the flames away from himself and Hammond. At the same time Hammond was still giving battle to the encircling enemy fighters. But the fire burned through the floor of the aircraft and the observer was forced to climb out of his cockpit and straddle the fuselage. Despite his severe wounds and perilous position, he held on to his machine gun and when another attacking triplane, thinking them finished, came in too close, Hammond calmly shot him down in flames. The five remaining Fokkers drew off warily.

By this time much of the fabric had been burned away from the left wing of the plane, and McLeod's right arm and shoulder had been badly scorched. Still he managed to maintain control over the burning machine. Ahead, through pain-clouded eyes, he could see the tangled barbed and the trenches of the British front line. There lay safety, if only he could stretch out the glide of his faltering craft.

Then the Fokkers made a final attack. Hammond, wounded for the sixth time, lost his balance and only prevented himself from falling through the bottom of the cockpit by hanging on to the machine gun mounting. The ground was coming up fast now and McLeod managed to bring the plane out of its steep sideslip, just as the wheels struck the ground heavily. The circling Germans fired one last burst into the wreckage and drew off. McLeod was thrown clear of the burning plane by the impact, but Hammond, now unconscious from loss of blood, was trapped in the flames which by now were licking at the load of bombs strapped beneath the lower wing. Although an explosion was imminent, and despite his four wounds, the Canadian staggered back into the inferno and dragged his observer to safety. They had just reached the shelter of a shell hole when the bombs exploded, and a metal fragment, striking McLeod, gave him his fifth wound. He fell in a faint across Hammond's prone body just as British troops rushed from their trenches and dragged the two into a dugout. German shells were now dropping all around the plane and it was several hours before the two gravely wounded airmen could be evacuated to a field hospital. It was some time before McLeod regained consciousness. When he did, he was told that he had been awarded the Victoria Cross for his day's work. For his part in the action Hammond won a bar to his Military Cross.

Both men recovered from their wounds but McLeod was still weak when sent home to Canada after his investiture at Buckingham Palace. Winnipeg gave him a hero's welcome. But on November 6, 1918, less than a week before the war ended, the boy who had survived so much died, the victim of an influenza epidemic.

The German pilot blinked confusedly behind his heavy flying goggles, as he tried to identify the plane approaching from the direction of the British lines. There was no doubt that it was British, for the red, white, and blue cocades stood out prominently against the khaki fabric. And it was clearly a two-seater, and therefore a high priority target which would not offer too much resistance to an ambitious young Albatross pilot out to make a name for himself. British two-seaters had been having a particular trying time during these early months of 1917, for many of them were now obsolete, greatly outclassed by the new German fighters. But this one? It had an underslung lower wing, its nose was long, and even from this distance, the businesslike way the observer swung his Lewis gun indicated a veteran crew. Then the identity of the plane registered in the German pilot's memory. With a confident smile, he tipped his sharp-nosed fighter up onto one wing and peeled off in a dive towards the Britisher.

He had identified the plane as a Bristol Fighter. This plane was nothing to worry about. It had been roundly defeated by the flyers of von Richthofen's flying circus when it had first appeared a few weeks earlier. Confidence grew within the German pilot as the British plane loomed larger in his ring sight. "A few short bursts," he thought, "and it will be all over."

But something strange happened. The British plane, instead of swinging its tail to meet the attack with the rear gun, in the conventional manner of two-seaters, had dropped one wing and banked around to face the German. Tracers flickered past the fuselage of the black-crossed fighter. The two planes shot past each other, and it was the two-seater that gained the vital altitude first, to turn and plunge like a pursuit plane on the Albatross. In a few seconds, it was all over. The Albatross was in a power spin, shedding long strips of fabric from its bullet-torn wings as it plunged towards the earth far below. High overhead, while his observer pounded him on the back, a young man named Andrew McKeever, from Listowel, Ontario, watched the falling plane grimly. It was his first victory.

McKeever was 22 when he reported for duty with No. 22 Squadron on the western front in May, 1917. He had been sent overseas with an infantry unit in 1915 and had first seen action as a sniper in the Ypres Salient. After repeated applications, he was finally transferred to the RFC and won his wings at Hounslow, England. The victory over the Albatross came on June 21, 1917.

The Bristol Fighter had just replaced the older RE-8 two-seater at No. 22 Squadron, but the new plane was regarded with deep suspicion by the pilots. The first Bristol patrol had almost been wiped out by enemy fighters, and pilots were afraid that the plane was a dud. But McKeever accepted the Bristol as a high performance machine. He set out at once to prove that its bad reputation was ill-founded.

As his observer McKeever picked a keen-eyed gunner named Sergeant L. F. Powell, who remained with the Canadian throughout his combat service. Together they flew and fought like a pair of demons during the early days of 1917, when the Germans were rushing up reinforcements to try and stem the British advance on the western front. The pair were forced to concentrate on ground targets in the area, since the Allies had achieved superiority in the air. But as the stunned Germans reacted, sending in fresh squadrons to replace those decimated by the British, the tempo of air fighting increased greatly. From June

20 to 27, McKeever shot down four enemy aircraft, all in one patrol. It was early in the morning and McKeever had attacked a German two-seater. His first burst set the German plane afire, then he heard Powell's gun hammering and, turning, saw seven Albatros scouts bearing down on them.

McKeever headed the Bristol for the safety of the British lines, and in the running fight, shot down two of the attacking fighters while Powell sent another spinning into the ground. McKeever was awarded the Military Cross for this exploit, and in August a bar was added to the Cross for another triple victory.

But the most memorable day for the Bristol team was on November 30, 1917. The Battle of Passchendaele had ground to a bloody halt in the mud of Flanders where thousands of Canadians had died in a fruitless attempt to breach the German line. At a cost of 24,000 casualties, the tiny village had finally been captured. Although this was hailed as a major victory, the German front was still intact when, 40 miles to the south, history was made at a place called Cambrai.

On November 20, Sir Julian Byng, the commander of the British Third Army, risked his professional career by using tanks against the Hindenburg Line for the first time without any preceding artillery barrage. Surprise was achieved and, since the ground at Cambrai was dry, unlike the soupy morass of Flanders, the 381 tanks rolled easily through the German line. A tremendous gap was torn in the line and a good deal of ground captured. But there were no reserves available to exploit the new gains and, ten days later, it was evident that the enemy was preparing a counter-offensive to regain the lost ground.

British army intelligence desperately needed information about enemy activities, so McKeever and Powell volunteered to fly a reconnaissance mission. It was an assignment fraught with danger. Several other planes had gone out for the same purpose and failed to return.

The day was wet and the cloud base was less than 1,00 feet when McKeever and Powell took off for the 60-mile trip from their base to Cambrai. Steering a compass course through a heavy rain squall, McKeever dropped down through the heavy clouds to find he had hit his destination right on the nose. While McKeever flew contours, dropping into hollows in the terrain to escape detection, Powell made notes on German troop formations moving along the fields and roads, which were just visible through the patchy fog.

With the observations completed, McKeever was climbing away for the trip home when suddenly the darkening sky was lit by a tremendous gush of flame. A chance shell from the Allied artillery positions had touched off a secret ammunition dump that had escaped even Powell's sharp eyes. In the sudden flash of fire McKeever saw hundreds of German soldiers trying to subdue the flames of the burning depot. Without a moment's delay, he dived for the ammunition dump, harassing the fire fighters with bombs and machine gun fire. He had no sooner started his attack when tracer bullets lashed his plane and, turning, he saw German machines lunging at him. His opponents were two bright red two-seater Rumplers and seven Albatros scouts. Pulling back the control stick to gain altitude, McKeever turned to meet the attack, a manoeuvre that caught the Germans by surprise. They had expected the lone Bristol to turn and run from such a vastly superior force.

McKeever met the leader head-on and pumped a ten-shot burst into him. As the German plane zoomed over their top wing, Powell raked it with his Lewis gun and the enemy plane twisted onto its back and fell in flames. Another Albatros crossed McKeever's gun sight and he riddled it with bullets. The plane staggered and fell off into a dive at full power. The first two were still falling when McKeever and Powell downed a third German plane, all within 10 seconds.

Stunned by the savage counter-attack, the six remaining German planes closed up and pressed in to attack as a unit. Again McKeever found black crosses in his sights and sent down one of the two-seaters with a single burst. As the scouts roared past, Powell hammered it with his Lewis gun. It glided away, its engine dead.

Then, almost simultaneously, McKeever ran out of ammunition and Powell's gun was smashed by a Spandau slug and rendered useless. A fragment of metal gashed Powell's cheek and another cut through McKeever's flying boot, grazing his leg. Hundreds of bullets ripped in their now defenceless plane. McKeever put the Bristol in a steep side-slip, making it appear as though his plane were out of control. The manoeuvre temporarily fooled his attackers, and they drew off. But just above the tree tops, McKeever levelled off and roared into the fog towards home. Using a row of trees along a main highway to screen him from the air, he hedgehopped towards the Allied lines. It was then that he realized how immediate was the danger to the Allied advance, for, as they neared the front, huge formations of German tanks, guns, and assault troops could be seen hidden in the woods and valleys. The enemy soldiers poured volleys of bullets into the badly damaged Bristol as it roared past, just above their heads. But the sturdy plane absorbed the punishment and survived the trip home.

Back at the aerodrome, a disappointed McKeever found that his information had come too late. The German attack had already begun and all the ground won by the brilliant tank attack ten days earlier was lost. McKeever was awarded the Distinguished Service Order for his brilliant exploits however, while Powell received the Distinguished Conduct Medal. Even if they had brought their information back in time to forestall the German counter-offensive, there is considerable doubt that anything could have been done, for the forces on hand were insufficient to meet the strong attack launched by the Germans.

In January, 1918, McKeever parted from his friend Powell to take over command of a training school in England. When the war ended later that year, he resigned from the RAF. McKeever possessed a rare combination of executive ability and flying skill and his postwar future seemed assured, for he had been offered the job of manager of a big new civilian aerodrome near Minneola, New York. But, as in the case of Barker and McElroy, Fate intervened. On Christmas Day, 1919, while driving between Listow and Stratford en route to his new job, Andrew McKeever's car skidded on an icy road, and he was fatally injured.

The Duellist

There was a murmur of astonishment among the officers and fashionably dressed ladies assembled at Buckinginham Palace that warm August day in 1917, as the name of William Avery Bishop was called for the second time. Some minutes earlier the young Canadian, wearing the wings of a pilot of the Royal Flying Corps on his trim tunic, had stood at rigid attention as His Majesty, King George the Fifth, pinned the Military Cross to that tunic just below the wings. Now, as a staff officer read the citation, the King selected another medal from a plush-lined box and pinned the Distinguished Service Order beside the Military Cross. It was not a common occurrence to see one man, presented, on the same day, with two of the highest awards the Empire could bestow. But this was not the end, for a moment later, the herald again called : "Captain William Avery Bishop, No. 60 Squadron, Royal Flying Corps...."

LCol W.A. (Billy) Bishop, V.C., in Lt. Quinn's studio, circa 1918-19, London, England.
Canada. Dept. of National Defence / National Archives of Canada / PA-006318

Silence fell over the gallery. This was unheard of. Three medals in one day? And the third one? His Majesty was "graciously pleased" to bestow on Captain Bishop the Victoria Cross. The King leaned forward to pin the bronze cross to the already resplendent tunic of the twenty-three-year-old Canadian. Only Bishop and the aide standing at the King's side heard the monarch's amused comment: "You have been making a nuisance of yourself out there, haven't you Captain?"

It was a typically British understatement. From March to August, 1917, in a period of less than six months, Billy Bishop had shot down a total of forty-seven enemy planes. Before his career in France ended with the Armistice in November, 1918, he would raise that total to seventy-two German planes, the second highest score of any pilot in the Royal Air Force.

Bishop was born on February 8, 1894. His father was the Registrar for York County, Ontario, and the family made their home in Owen Sound. Since he was an unusually active boy, his parents decided that military discipline would be good for him, and he was enrolled as an officer cadet in the Royal Military College at Kingston. After graduation, he served with the Mississauga Horse of Toronto for a time, then, in 1915, joined the ranks of the famous Canadian Mounted Rifles, the alma mater of many of Canada's cavalrymen-turned-aviators. He went overseas with the regiment and saw action in the battles of 1915. But Bishop, like Barker, wearied of the muddy trenches and applied for a transfer to the Royal Flying Corps.

Bishop's first tour of duty also paralleled Barker's. Since he was known as a marksman with either rifle or machine gun, Air Force Headquarters assigned him to a two-seater as an observer-gunner. This type of flying merely whetted Bishop's appetite, for after four months of it he applied for training as a pilot.

His first assignment on graduation was to a Zeppelin defence squadron in England. While it offered the eager young flyer little in the way of actual battle experience, the assignment, which entailed constant patrolling at high altitudes, did allow him to perfect his flying skill before he was sent to the front.

Bishop arrived in France like a pent-up whirlwind. At last he had reached the battle zone. All the frustrations of lonely patrols over the English Channel were just a memory. He had been sent to No. 60 Squadron, one of the most famous units in the Royal Flying Corps. The squadron was heavily engaged in the bitter air fighting that was raging over Flanders. Bishop had arrived at a time that has been described as the most disastrous period in the history of the RFC. It was the spring of 1917: "Bloody April."

The young Canadian was flushed with pride at being assigned to so famous a unit. It was with 60 Squadron that England's famous Albert Ball had scored so many victories.

Bishop was disappointed to learn that Ball had just been sent back to England for a rest; he had followed the young Englishman's career closely and yearned for a chance to discuss combat tactics with him. With Ball away, the Canadian did the next best thing: he pestered everyone in the squadron with questions about Ball's style of air fighting.

His investigation of Captain Ball's tactics revealed an approach to combat that, with some modification, suited Bishop's temperament. Ball was daring to the point of recklessness. Time after time he attacked superior formations, on the theory that the element of surprise would offset the enemy's advantage in numbers. Bishop approved of the principle of utilizing surprise, but whereas Ball would descend like a whirlwind from his vantage point of height, Bishop preferred to make greater use of his own talent with a machine gun. A deadly shot, he would stalk his quarry for some time before swooping in for a single burst of fire which often reached its target before the enemy pilot was even aware of Bishop's presence.

Number 60 Squadron flew the manoeuvrable little French-built Nieuport 17, a single-seater, powered by a rotary engine and armed with a single Lewis gun fixed on a mount on the top wing. Bishop liked the plane and especially liked the gun, which he had mastered during his days with the cavalry. From its mounting, the gun could be fired straight ahead, over the arc of the propeller, or it could be pulled back into the cockpit to fire straight up at enemy machines passing overhead. Bishop cherished the weapon to the point where he refused to allow the squadron's armourers to handle the gun. He undertook the care and maintenance of his own weapon, personally loading every round into the forty-seven-shot magazines. He practised with the weapon whenever he had a free moment. To improve his reflexes and his aim, he often took empty tin cans into the air with him, throwing them from the plane and trying to riddle them with bullets as they fell to earth.

His first victory, over a new Albatros D-3, was scored several days after joining the squadron. It was a notable success for a new man, since not many of the Albatros aircraft were appearing in the victory claims of the RFC during this period. March passed into April and the furious onslaught of the fast, new German planes reached its peak. British planes fell in ever increasing numbers— yet Bishop during this same period scored eleven victories, six of which were over deadly D-3's.

It was apparent to everyone in 60 Squadron that they had found a suitable replacement for Albert Ball. Both men specialized in lone patrols, when, far behind German lines, they would hover at extreme altitudes, watching for German formations heading for the front, Then the fast swoop, the stuttering roar of the machine gun, and another black-crossed fighter would spin into the earth.

Bishop had now achieved a status that, he felt, warranted a distinctive trademark. Once again he looked to the man he most admired, Albert Ball. The young English ace had marked his plane by attaching a streamlined spinner— probably from the propeller of a fallen Albatros—to his propeller and painting it red. It was not long before German pilots all along the western front knew and feared this red-nosed Nieuport. Bishop liked the idea and adapted it to his own plane, only changing the colour of the spinner to blue.

Despite similarities, Ball and Bishop differed considerably in their approach to fighting. Ball was a madcap who ignored enemy guns and bullets in pressing home his attack. His very fury seemed to be the main factor in his success. Bishop, on the contrary, was a clean, precise duellist, and a crack shot. Always cool-headed in the air, he simply out-flew and out-shot his opponent. Only rarely did he display the fighting rage of Ball. One such occasion he has himself related in one of his books.

He had been assigned the job of providing air support for a British ground attack. As he was circling above no man's land, he saw a party of British troops pinned down by a German machine gun nest. A cold fury came over him as he watched the bullets from the hidden German gun send the tiny, khaki-clad figures of British Tommies spinning and falling into the mud. Searching for the enemy pillbox, Bishop spotted it, hidden in the wreckage of an old house. Shoving the nose of his plane down, he dived towards the pillbox, his gun sending a stream of bullets into the cluster of grey-clad German infantrymen. He emptied an entire magazine into the emplacement, reloaded, and attacked again and again. Finally the gun was silent and the Tommies below resumed their attack.

Undated photo shows a Royal Aircraft Factory S.E. 5a fighter aircraft. The most successful R.A. Factory product, the S.E. 5 family was designed to be easy to fly and, if not as manoeuvrable as its contemporaries, it was still a formidable fighter. Developed from the S.E. 5, which entered operational service in France in April 1917, the S.E. 5a featured a more powerful 200-hp Hispano-Suiza V-8 engine, giving top speed of 138 mph, service ceiling of 22,000 ft. and endurance of three hours. It was 20 ft. 11 in. long, spanned 26 ft. 7 1/2 in., stood 9 ft. 6 in. high, weighed 1,400 lb. empty and a maximum 1,955 lb. on takeoff. It carried one pilot—some were modified as two-place trainers—one forward-firing Vickers .303-in. machine gun with interruptor gear, one flexible Lewis .303-in. machine gun over the centre section of the upper wing, and as many as four 25-lb. bombs. 5,205 S.E. 5s and 5as were built.
Department of National Defence/AH-194

Bishop was relentless and fearless in battle. He flew incessantly, in all types of weather. If he could find no aerial targets to attack, he contented himself with trench-strafing and balloon-busting. His exploits were now well known on both sides of the Atlantic. Back in Canada, the magic of Bishop's name encouraged other young Canadians to seek out a military career in the air. By his very brilliance Bishop was far from being the typical airman, but to the British he seemed representative of Canada's youth. *The Times* of London, in its history of the war, used the example of Bishop's career to illustrate the popular belief that Canadians were "born to fly." *The Times* observed: "The British authorities early came to realize the special adaptability and initiative of the Canadian young man." Bishop became one of "those Canadians [who] from the beginning of the war took a prominent part in the work of both the Royal Flying Corps and the Royal Naval Air Service."

Billy Bishop was yet to have his most memorable day, however. It all started just before dawn on June 2, 1917. The flying field was still in darkness when Bishop rose from his bed, pulled his clothing on over his pyjamas, and left his quarters. After a brief stop at the mess hall for a gulp of scalding tea and some army biscuits, he whistled for his dog Nig and walked to the nearby hangars. Inside the hangar Bishop's mechanic, Corporal Walter Bourne, was fussing over the engine of the Canadian's sleek, blue-nosed Nieuport. "All right, Corporal, roll her out."

Seated in the cockpit, Bishop pulled an oil-stained leather helmet over his tousled, light brown hair, at the same making a last minute cockpit check. Then he nodded his head and the mechanic swung the prop. The engine wheezed, then burst into life as gas flooded the cylinders. At Bishop's wave, the mechanics pulled the chocks from under the wheels. Corporal Bourne's shouted "Good luck, sir!" was lost in the roar of the motor as the plane lunged through the open door of the hangar and swung off the field into the darkness, heading for the grey eastern horizon.

Hedgehopping to avoid anti-aircraft fire, Bishop headed deep into German territory. Fifteen miles behind the German front line, an airfield was receiving the first telephone alarm that a single British fighter had crossed the line at dawn and was heading their way. Officers shouted orders and sweating mechanics wheeled seven fighters from their hangars and swung the props to warm the engines.

It was too late. Over the trees that bordered the field, Bishop's plane burst on the scene like a hawk on a chicken coop. At an altitude of less than one hundred feet, he swooped down on the line of fighters, his Lewis gun stitching the wings and motors of the grounded planes. One Albatros began to roll forward in a take-off and Bishop pointed one wing at the ground and spun around after it. His gun stuttered sparingly and fifteen bullets thudded into the cockpit and engine of the taxiing plane, just as it lifted from the field. It dug in one wing and ground-looped itself into a pile of wreckage.

A second plane had started down the field and Bishop pulled his control stick back into his stomach, achieving altitude for a second attack. He roared after the moving plane and this time it took thirty bullets. The enemy machine piled into the trees at the end of the runway. Then numbers began to tell. While Bishop was occupied with the first two, another pair of Albatroses scooted down field and soared into the air, banking left and right to avoid him. Climbing fast as he reloaded his Lewis gun, Bishop closed with the nearest, which had reached an altitude of 1,000 feet. Under the whiplash of Bishop's gun, pieces came away from the German plane, and it crashed less than three hundred yards from where it had taken off.

By this time ground fire and bullets from the fighters had turned Bishop's plane into a tattered wreck, but he lunged after the fourth Albatros and emptied a full drum of ammunition into it. As the plane tumbled wildly to escape the bullets, Bishop, noting other enemy planes taking off from the field, decided to call it a day. Reaction to the intense excitement set in, and on the flight home he had to fight dizziness and nausea. Four enemy planes chased him all the way to the lines, but he managed to outfly them and bring his heavily damaged plane to a safe landing at his own field. He was greeted by a crowd of excited airmen; they had learned of the fight from observers in the British balloon line who had seen the whole affair from their swaying baskets. When Bishop was asked how many machines he had shot down, he replied with unconscious modesty: "Only three. One got away."

Later investigation revealed that he had severely damaged a number of other planes on the ground and had wounded the pilot of the fourth German fighter which had "got away." Bishop's report of the mission against the enemy aerodrome was carefully scrutinized and substantiated before, on August 11, 1917, he was informed by the Commander of the air contingents in France that he had been awarded the Victoria Cross—the first Canadian airman to receive the decoration. Bishop quietly thanked his superiors and left the squadron office.

Fellow pilots, curious as to why he had been summoned, received no satisfaction from Bishop, who walked back to the flight line where Bourne was working on his plane. After a moment of conversation about the repairs, Bishop added, almost as an afterthought: "We've won the Victoria Cross."

Bishop was sent back to England to receive the medal along with the Distinguished Service Order and the Military Cross which had been awarded him for earlier exploits. His record now showed forty-seven confirmed victories. As one of the senior RFC aces still alive, he was now too valuable to be risked in the daily rough and tumble of air fighting. Besides the loss of his experience if he were killed, another consideration was the crushing blow to civilian morale that would inevitably follow. Britain had recently suffered the loss of Albert Ball, who had been killed in action. Secretary of State for Air, Winston Churchill, was not going to allow the death of another hero to spread a pall of gloom over England. So despite Bishop's vigorous protests, he was ordered to leave the front and go home to Canada on leave.

After completing his leave and returning to England, Bishop found himself posted to a training command. Like Barker, Bishop rebelled, but in a more restrained manner. By the spring of 1918, his repeated pleas for a return to active duty were heard and he was sent to France to command a new squadron, No. 85, equipped with the fast, heavily armed SE-5 fighters. Since squadron command were forbidden to fly, Bishop's job was to "fly a desk," sending other men into battle while he remained on the ground. It was a task quite alien to his personality, but orders were orders.

New squadrons were now being given a little more time to familiarize themselves with terrain and tactics before going directly into action. Bishop used his experience as a flight instructor to skirt the regulation which kept him on ground. He managed to obtain permission to lead his new men in daily practice formation flights, teaching them the value of tight aerial discipline and showing them how to use their eyes. Though airmen were required to have perfect eyesight, Bishop, the lone wolf of the past, knew only too well how easy it was to fail to see an enemy fighter lurking under a cloudbank or riding high in the sun, shielded by the blinding rays.

Each day he would lead his entire squadron over the lines, and later, back at the air base, would question each man carefully about what he had seen. "Didn't see a thing, sir," said one new man. Bishop promptly gave a detailed account of the types and position of almost a dozen German planes that had passed their formation during the flight. With lessons like these, he hoped to give these young flyers a chance of survival.

However, while conducting these instruction patrols which stressed the value of working as a team, Bishop still carried out his solo patrol work. Often, after leading his squadron safely back to their own lines, he would drop out of formation and vanish. He knew that the time for lessons was growing short.

The squadron would soon be thrown into the fighting, and he would be forced to return to his desk.

It was during this period that Billy Bishop established his reputation as one of the greatest solo duellists of the war. In twelve days he shot down a total of twenty-five enemy aircraft, a record that few, if any, combat pilots ever equalled. By comparison, it took the leading American ace, Eddie Rickenbacker, almost a year to score an equal number of victories. On his last day of front line flying, with orders in his pocket to leave at once to join the staff of the Air Ministry in London, Bishop made his final solo offensive patrol behind the German lines and shot down five enemy aircraft.

After the war, Bishop was sent back to Canada to help organize the Canadian Air Force. Then he left the service and tried his hand at business, but he missed flying and did not remain too long in any particular field. He proved to be an able writer, and his books on aerial warfare are considered models of their kind. At one time there was a suggestion that a documentary motion picture about his life be made, but unfortunately it never got beyond the planning stage.

When the Second World War began Bishop again offered his services. His dream was to be given command of a fighter wing. Again he was considered too valuable to risk, and again it was Winston Churchill who refused his request for active duty. Churchill gently reminded him of a similar plea he had made in 1918 and told him truthfully that would be of more value to the war effort in recruiting the young men needed to man the air fleets of the Second World War. Reluctantly, Air Marshal William A. Bishop, VC, DSO, MC, agreed with the great statesman.

The Black Flight

A resolution had been forming for some time in the mind of Raymond Collishaw of Nanaimo, B.C. The idea had begun to germinate when the twenty-two-year-old sailor had first arrived in England in 1915, ready to join one of His Majesty's vessels of war. Now his mind was made up; and when Ray Collishaw made up his mind, he seldom bothered with second thoughts. He immediately put pen to paper and set out his reasons for asking the Lords of the Admirality to consider favourably his request for a transfer from duty as a ship's deck officer to training as a pilot in the Royal Naval Air Service.

It was a radical step for a young man fully qualified in ship handling and navigation. Collishaw had already worked his way up from the lower deck status of a seaman to that of an officer. All his early life had been spent mastering the intricacies of seamanship. Born close to the sea on Vancouver Island, his boyhood had been coloured with images of sea voyages and ships. At the age of fifteen, he turned his dreams into reality by signing on with a fisheries patrol vessel. The young Collishaw found himself thoroughly at home on the windswept decks of the small patrol boats plying the waters off the B.C. coast. He learned the rough give and take of shipboard life and in a few years had achieved the position of second mate aboard a passenger vessel making scheduled trips to Alaska. Following that, his ability earned him a berth on one of the exploratory expeditions in the Antarctic. When the war started in 1914, he appeared to be all set for a career as a ship's officer. Had he remained true to his first love, the sea, his subsequent history would have been different. With his personal magnetism, sense of duty, and initiative, he would probably have soon achieved the ultimate ambition of all sailors, the command of his own ship.

As it was, one day, shortly after his arrival in England, he saw an airplane in flight. The sight of this new weapon of war fired his imagination; he decided to become a pilot. He enlisted with the Royal Naval Air Service in Canada in 1915. The RNAS had started a limited recruiting programme in this country, whereby air crews were recruited providing that each man paid the cost of his own flying training. Collishaw accepted and took pre-flight training at the Curtiss Flying School in Toronto. The School closed before he completed the course, and the RNAS shipped him overseas to complete his training, under RNAS instruction, in England. By January, 1916, he was a qualified pilot with the Royal Naval Air Service and was flying patrols over the ports along the English Channel, looking for Zeppelins and U-boats. It was a dull job, with little to offer that would satisfy Collishaw's craving for action. So the young sailor welcomed the change when, in August, he was transferred to No. 3 Naval Wing, the first strategic bombing force ever formed. The wing was to operate from fields in the Vosges section of north-eastern France and was to attack selected industrial targets far inside Germany, at the limit of the bomber's range. As preparation for this role, the squadron was sent to Manston, Kent, to train. While at Manston, Collishaw and a friend struck up an acquaintance with two girls in the neighbouring village. The four had planned a double date one night when orders came through for the squadron to move to France. There was no telephone connection with the young ladies so Collishaw decided to deliver his regrets personally. He took one of the squadron's planes up, intending to drop a note in the back garden of his girlfriend's home. Unfortunately his engine failed as he swooped over the house and the plane crashed, smashing several garden walls and ripping out the rear wall of the girl's home. Collihaw was uninjured, but, as he said later: "The neighbours were not very pleased."

Pilots with Sopwith F.1 Camel aircraft of No. 203 Squadron RAF, from left, Lt. A.T. Whealy and Squadron Commander Raymond Collishaw, of Nanaimo, B.C. Photo taken at Allonville, France, in July 1918. Canada: Dept. of National Defence/National Archives of Canada/PA-002789.

Collishaw's first major combat mission was an attack on the Mauser rifle factory at Oberndorf on October 12, 1916. The formation of French and British bombers included fourteen Canadians in its personnel. This history-making raid was not an easy operation, and the force had to fight its way to the target, battling successive waves of German fighters. The raiding force was made up of two-seater day-bombers (Sopwith one-and-a-half strutters) escorted by Sopwith Pup fighters, less than twenty planes in all. The mission was a success despite severe attacks from enemy fighters on the formation. Collishaw, who was flying an escort plane, scored his first victory by shooting the wings off an enemy scout while defending the bombers. Less than two weeks later he boosted his total by two when he shot down two of the fast new Albatros D-3's, known among British flyers as "widow makers."

Collishaw's air fighting tactics lacked the duellist's virtuosity of Barker or Bishop. They both possessed a rare combination of marksmanship and flying ability, but what the British Columbian lacked in skill with a machine gun he made up with a remarkable ferocity of attack. He would lunge close to his opponents, braving heavy defensive fire or a close-range shot that could not miss. He was the Jack Dempsey of the air, wading through a barrage of blows to deliver the knockout punch. As a result, his machine often came home riddled with bullets and he himself missed death by inches countless times. His first narrow escape came on December 27, 1916, when his plane was shot down, the engine and cowling punctured in a dozen places by bullets. With power gone, Collishaw made a dead stick landing and escaped unhurt.

A second close shave occurred after the wing moved to Ochey, near the big aircraft replacement centre of Toul, to be closer to its main target, the German steel industry of the Saar basin. Collishaw was asked to pick up a new plane one day. He left Toul in the plane, a two-seater, without a rear gunner. On his way back to the base he was attacked. During the fight, a bullet smashed his goggles and he was temporarily blinded. In a bid to lose the enemy planes, he dived away—into German territory. Soon he was alone, and, at low altitude, swung his plane towards the French lines. An aerodrome appeared and Collishaw, exhausted and still half blind from the stunning blow of the bullet, landed his plane. He was taxiing among the parked aircraft when, with a shock, he suddenly noticed they were all marked with black crosses. He had landed by mistake at a German drome. Collishaw gunned the motor and roared down the field, bullets digging into the ground behind him. His plane lifted just in time, clipping the tops of two trees.

On February 1, 1917, Collishaw was transferred to No. 3 Naval Squadron and on March 4, he raised his victory total when he shot down another Albatros

D-3. His operations on the western front made Collishaw something of an authority on the aircraft turned out by the Sopwith factory in England. Early in his career, he flew the reliable Sopwith one-and-a-half strutter. At the beginning of his service as a fighter pilot, his plane was the Sopwith Pup, the forerunner of a distinguished line of Sopwith models, and, for many pilots, the favourite of the family. Designed to combat the Fokker Eindekker menace, the Pup came into action late in 1916, when the Germans had replaced the Eindekker with faster, more powerful models. Surprisingly, though it was one of the better fighters of that year, the shabbily equipped Royal Flying Corps turned the Pup down, and it went to naval squadrons. Underpowered, and designed to fight a different foe, it performed yeoman service against the powerful Albatros fighters. Collishaw learned much about air combat tactics in the Pup, which responded easily to his touch and endeared itself to him.

On April Fool's Day, 1917, the Navy played a nasty trick on the Germans and introduced Ray Collishaw to the plane that would make him famous, the rakish-looking Sopwith Triplane. Lieutenant Ray Collishaw was handed his

Undated photo shows a Sopwith Triplane on the flight line. This aircraft has the standard 110-hp Clerget engine and rarer twin Vickers .303-in. machine gun armament -- most Triplanes carried only one -- mounted atop the fuselage and synchronized to fire between the propeller blades. The Triplane, which debuted in prototype form on May 28, 1916, was initially ordered for Britain's Royal Flying Corps but an interservice swap meant the 140 built served exclusively with the Royal Naval Air Service. B Flight of No. 10 Naval Squadron, manned entirely Canadians, was known as the Black Flight; its five aircraft, painted overall black except for squadron and rudder markings, were dubbed Black Maria, Black Death, Black Roger, Black Prince and Black Sheep. Between May and July 1917, they shot down 87 enemy aircraft. The Triplane was replaced by the Sopwith Camel in November 1917. Top speed was 117 mph, service ceiling was 20,500 ft. and endurance was 2 hrs. 45 mins. The Triplane was 18 ft. 10 in. long, spanned 26 ft. 6 in., stood 10 ft. 6 in. tall and weighed 1,101 lb. empty and a maximum 1,541 lb. at takeoff. Department of National Defence/AH493 transfer orders that day and told to report to No. 10 Naval Squadron as the commander of B Flight. The squadron was being sent to the Flanders front to help the hard-pressed Royal Flying Corps.

This was "Bloody April." Baron Manfred von Richthofen's flying circus had gone into action in January as an untried group of fledglings. Now they were all aces, thanks to the superiority of their equipment, a fact not realized by one correspondent, who called them "cold-eyed killers." Most of the machines used by the RFC were not adequate to cope with the German planes, and for a time the Germans enjoyed complete aerial dominance. The RFC, at the mercy of the British Government's Air Board, which was still trying to standardize aircraft design to cut costs, was unable to get the variety of machines it needed. The aircraft situation became so bad that General Trenchard, the commander of the RFC, told his superiors: "I want to beat the Boche in *this* war, not the next."

Number 10 Squadron, RNAS, had just been re-equipped with the Sopwith Triplane, which had passed its final production tests almost a year earlier. Despite its high performance record, the triplane had been rejected by the RFC, probably because of its unusual appearance. Consequently, most of the three-wingers went into action as naval aircraft on Channel patrol. Sopwith engineers had had no precedent to guide them when they designed the Tripe. They had wanted a plane that would incorporate maximum lift in a short wingspan, plus the ability to turn inside the turning radius of contemporary German planes. The result was the triplane, a light ship with a fast rate of climb and a ceiling of 20,500 feet. Armed with a single machine gun synchronized to fire through the propeller arc, the triplane had a top speed of 115 miles per hour at 15,000 feet. A Sopwith Triplane, probably from Collishaw's squadron, was credited with shooting down and wounding the youngest brother of the Red Knight, Lothar von Richthofen, who was an ace in his own right with forty victories.

As losses mounted on the western front, the desperate RFC was forced to take another look at the plane they had turned down and borrowed a squadron from the RNAS to fill the gaps left by the Spandau guns of the German fighters. The squadron selected, No. 10, boasted some of the best fighter pilots in the RNAS, men handpicked by Naval Headquarters. Among them was Ray Collishaw.

Collishaw was delighted with his new command. B Flight was composed entirely of Canadians: Flight Sub-Lieutenants Ellis Reid of Toronto, J. E. Sharman of Winnipeg, J. E. Nash of Hamilton, and W. M. Alexander of Toronto.

Many German squadrons had adopted the practice of the Richthofen circus and were painting their planes with vivid colours and insignia. Collishaw decided that his all-Canadian flight should also have a distinctive trademark to distinguish them from the Army's RFC squadrons. After consulting his men it was decided to paint every plane in the flight jet black. With light-hearted bravado they dubbed their formation the "Black Flight." Collishaw's plane was "Black Maria"; Reid flew "Black Roger"; Sharman was in "Black Death"; Nash christened his plane "Black Sheep"; and Alexander assumed an air of royalty with "Black Prince."

There were, no doubt, a few covert sneers among the jaded and battle-weary RFC pilots when these cocky young navy flyers arrived on the scene in their funereal triplanes and brave *noms de guerre*. But the sneers vanished quickly when the group went into action, for the Black Flight proved to be one of the most successful air fighting teams of the war.

On the morning of June 27, 1917, four jet-black triplanes roared across the bumpy pasture land that was the landing field of No. 10 Naval Squadron, climbed at a steep angle, and slanted their way towards the shell-scarred Flanders battlefield. Ostensibly this was a routine offensive patrol for the Black Flight. Actually the four Canadian flyers were setting out to pursue a vendetta with a certain German pilot who flew a vivid green Albatros fighter. Flight Leader Ray Collishaw and his three wingmates had a score to settle with the German.

The Black Flight had been in action almost three months. Through the darkest days of "Bloody April" the five Canadians seemed invulnerable, though disastrous casualties were being suffered by other British flying units. In their black triplanes they opposed the top German squadrons on the Flanders front and came away unscathed. Each had downed the required number of German planes to become an ace. By June 5, Collishaw had brought his personal score to thirteen with the destruction of an Albatros two-seater. The following day he shot down three Albatros D-3's in a single fight. Several other individual victories followed and on June 15 he downed three Halberstadt fighters and an LVG two-seater, bringing his victory tally to twenty-three, sixteen of them shot down in a twenty-seven-day period.

But the charmed life of the Black Flight could not last. On June 26 the Canadians, rushing to help a flight of British planes, ran head-on into the entire *Jagdstaffel* of von Richthofen. Despite the stiff odds, the five black triplanes held their own against the foremost squadron of the German Air Force. In the mêlée, Richthofen and his leading ace, Leutnant Karl Allmenroeder, whose thirty victories had won for him the ribbon of the Blue Max, Germany's highest decoration, pounced on the tail of Nash's "Black Sheep." It was Allmenroeder's guns which sent the black triplane crashing behind the German lines. Other members of the Black Flight, busy with their opponents, could do little but note this fact and mark Allmenroeder's all-green Albatros for a future reckoning. After an indecisive battle with the German formation the four surviving triplanes flew home. That night a pall of gloom hung over the usually gay billets of the Canadians. Nash had gone down pretty fast and it seemed probable that he was dead.

While badly shaken by the crash, Nash was actually not seriously hurt. German soldiers pulled him from the wreckage of his plane and took him prisoner. It was a custom among flyers to offer a downed foe a night's entertainment at the squadron mess before he was shipped away to the dreary life of a prison camp. Nash was lodged in a small cell near the Jasta 11 base at Marcke on the Ypres front. His wounds were treated and he was told he would spend the night there.

The next day, while Nash nursed his bruises and contemplated a dismal future as a prisoner of war, the Black Flight set out to find the German in the vivid green Albatros. They found their quarry leading a formation of Jasta 11 aircraft high over the German-held industrial city of Lille. The Albatros at the head of the vari-coloured formation acted like a magnet for the four black triplanes, but it was Collishaw who managed to break through the wildly manoeuvring German fighters and close in on the green ship. The Canadian attacked with a single purpose: to get the man who shot down Nash. Collishaw had no way, of knowing that Nash was still alive and almost within earshot of their roaring motors.

The green plane avoided Collishaw's charge with a fast wingover and the aerobatics of the two master flyers soon carried them clear of the main battle. It was no easy contest, for Allmenroeder was an accomplished aerial duelist. But the greater speed of his craft and its heavy motor were not fitted for such a fight. On the other hand, Collishaw's infighting tactics were aided by the easy manoeuvrability of his triplane, designed for exactly this type of action. Again and again the lighter British plane danced away from the faster German, gaining vital altitude each time they circled each other. Then Collishaw spotted an opening and rushed in. At point-blank range he fired a long burst into the fuselage of the Albatros which plunged to the ground.

Later that day, the tolling of a church bell caught Nash's attention as he waited in his tiny cell to be transported to the prison camp. From the barred window he saw a group of German officers accompanying a *coffin* into the nearby churchyard. The helmeted guard at his cell door, who could speak English, provided the explanation. The funeral, he said, was for Leutnant Karl Allmenroeder, "a very famous *Kanone* [ace] ... the man who shot you down yesterday."

This anecdote illustrates Collishaw's deep sense of responsibility for the men under his command. A group photograph of his squadron shows him, a smiling, stocky young man, standing with his wingmates. His hands rest on the shoulders of two of them, much like a proud eldest son among his younger brothers. It was this quality in his nature which made him react as he did to the shooting down of Nash. A former member of 203 Squadron, Collishaw's last command of the war, had this to say about him: "Most of the 'stars' were extremely conscientious about making sure they were given full credit for their victories. There was always a semi-official competition among the better flyers to top each other's scores. Collishaw wasn't like that. He seemed at times almost indifferent to confirmation of his victories. And one of his practices was to give away victories to new men. He felt that this bolstered their confidence and helped them to survive. If he and a rookie fired on the same plane, 'Collie' would always maintain it was the rookie's bullets that had got it." Thus, had Collishaw claimed his victories as jealously as other flyers, his official total of sixty, placing him third in the RAF, would have been considerably higher.

The Black Flight became a familiar sight over the tragic marshlands of Flanders. Between May and July the flight had destroyed the phenomenal total of eighty-seven enemy aircraft. Collishaw personally accounted for sixteen enemy losses in June alone. By the first week in July his personal score had risen to twenty-seven, and he was awarded the Distinguished Service Order. During that month, ten more enemy fighters fell before his guns.

It was during the same month, on July 15, that Collishaw had another narrow brush with death. It was on an offensive patrol over the German lines. His squadron tangled with a formation of German fighters, and Collishaw found an enemy aircraft riding his tail. Tracer bullets ripped into the wings and tail of his machine and his control wires parted. By using the motor and ailerons to compensate for controls that had been shot away, he managed to glide his crippled fighter to the safety of British lines, pancaking his plane into a muddy field. The plane was a total wreck, but Collishaw escaped unharmed.

He was back in the air again the next day and, on July 20, he was awarded the Distinguished Service Cross for shooting down three Albatros fighters in a single combat. Eight days later he was granted two months' leave in Canada.

Collishaw returned to France in October, 1917, and was given command of No. 13 Naval Squadron, a formation equipped with the Sopwith Camel. By this time the Black Flight had been disbanded, its members having been sent to different areas of the conflict. In his position as squadron commander, Collishaw found himself chained to a desk, facing an ever-mounting stack of paperwork. Even when he did manage to wade through this paper war, there were new restrictive orders issued by the High Command, prohibiting squadron commanders from flying combat patrols. Number 13 Squadron was a seaplane defence unit and the tempo of the war along the Belgian seacoast was slower than at the western front, where daily battles raged. Nevertheless, despite the paperwork and High Command's orders, Collishaw managed to shoot down two German seaplanes and a two-seater during his tour with the squadron.

On January 23, 1918, he was again transferred, this time to the post of commander of No. 3 Naval Squadron. Administrative duties kept him grounded until June, but when he again took to the air, he soon proved that he had not lost his touch, and three new Pfalz fighters fell before his guns.

At this time, the main threat to the British bid for aerial superiority was the new Fokker D-7, one of the finest airplanes to be developed during the First War. "Fokker fever" was taking a heavy toll of Allied pilots and a brace of D-7's almost ended the career of Collishaw. He was patrolling alone near the lines one day when he spotted a British plane in serious trouble. The plane, a Spad, had evidently become separated from its formation and, while trying to get home, had been jumped by a pair of high-flying Fokkers. Now the lone Britisher weaved and dodged frantically as he ran a gauntlet of tracer bullets that sparkled from the guns of the Fokkers. Collishaw was still some distance away, but he shoved the nose of his ship down to gain flying speed and sped to the rescue of the hemmed-in Spad. Still out of range, he saw the British plane spout smoke, then point its nose towards the ground far below.

The triumphant German planes zoomed up and split to the right and left, hoping to catch a second victim between their guns. Collishaw, hot with anger, gave them no chance to develop their attack. He plunged at the nearest Fokker head-on, and when the German broke right to avoid collision, the Canadian raked his floorboards. The turn of the German plane tightened into a spin and it went down. The second plane was now on Collishaw, its guns pounding. Bullets thudded and crashed into the light aluminum that covered the motor of the Camel but, again, the Nanaimo flyer closed to point-blank range and poured a volley into the German plane. It shed a gout of smoke and fell into a dive.

Collishaw had won, but whether he would live to talk about his victory was another matter. The bullet-riddled rotary engine of his plane coughed and fell silent, the prop windmilling without power. He was still over the German lines and a landing here meant capture. Gaining flying speed by diving, Collishaw expertly handled stick and rudder to glide the plane across the British lines to a crash landing.

A few days later, with a new plane, he was back again over the German lines on offensive patrols. Relentlessly, he built up his score until it reached sixty victories. By this time he had added a bar to his DSO and had been awarded the Distinguished Flying Cross. It was at this time that the RNAS and RFC were merged to become the Royal Air Force, and Collishaw's squadron, No. 3 Naval, was redesignated as No. 203 Squadron, RAF, a unit in which more than half the pilots were Canadian. On October 1, a little more than a month before the Armistice, Collishaw was promoted to the rank of lieutenant-colonel and ordered back to England to help form the new Canadian Air Force. He was one of about 450 Canadian flying officers in England when, at a special ceremony at Buckingham Palace, the colours for the new service were presented.

The war had ended, however, before Canada's Air Force could enter the fighting. Collishaw, along with thousands of other men, returned to his home, but his farewell to active service was only temporary. The guns may have been silent along the western front, but there was still a battle raging in the East. The Russian Revolution, at first hailed by western liberals as a triumph of democracy against the rule of a despot, had been snatched from the hands of the liberal forces by the Bolsheviks. Russian fought Russian in that most bitter of conflicts, civil war, as the Reds of Lenin struggled for supreme power against the White counterrevolution under the military leadership of Admiral Kolchak.

The western world viewed with alarm the growing power of the Bolsheviks and their doctrine of world revolution. Britain, mainly on the urging of Winston Churchill, sent men and machines to the White Russian Army. Led by General Denekin, the White Army was trying to push northwards from the Crimea into the heart of Russia. Collishaw, still attached to the RAF, returned to England in 1919 and found an exciting offer awaiting him: the command of a squadron whose job was to provide aerial support for Denekin's army. The Nanaimo flyer was now twenty-seven years of age and had seen enough military service to satisfy the average man's taste for action, but he readily accepted the new assignments. He then spent many days visiting a number of RAF units in Britain, hand-picking the men who would accompany him.

His new command, No. 47 Squadron, RAF, was a composite group of three flights of single-seater Camels and three flights of de Havilland 9 day-bombers. Collishaw made it practically all-Canadian, for fifty-three of the squadron's sixty-two officers came from Canada. Russia had always been an enigma to the people of the West and now, into this remote country that brooded alone on the eastern boundary of Europe, obscured further by the smoke of battle, Collishaw led his Canadians.

The squadron landed at Novorisisk, in southern Russia, and joined up with the forces of General Denekin. It acted as air support for three White Russian armies: the Kuban Cossacks, operating from a small city on the Volga known as Tsaritsyn, which was later named Stalingrad; the Don Cossacks, who operated in the territory between Stalingrad and Kharkov; and the Volunteer Army of the Ukraine. Collishaw's men were appalled at what they found. The fratricidal conflict lent new horror to the savagery of war. Prisoners were shot callously by both sides, and the fate of foreign mercenaries was even less gentle. The men of 47 Squadron soon learned that they could not expect to be treated as prisoners of war if they were forced to land behind enemy lines.

It was a strange, gypsy-like campaign for these battle-tested Canadians. Used to the static warfare that had existed along the western front for four years, they found themselves living the life of nomads, moving with Denekin's army from place to place, advancing or retreating with the ground forces.

By the autumn of 1919, Collishaw had established his headquarters at Krasnodar. At first a few enemy planes were encountered, piloted by German flyers. Collishaw was the first pilot serving with the White Army to score a victory on the southern Russian front. His victim was a familiar foe, a German Albatros D-5, its black crosses painted over with the red star of the Bolsheviks. Although it did not take long for Collishaw's crack pilots to dispose of the enemy air force, it was not a simple operation. Adventure was evenly distributed among the flyers of 47 Squadron. An incident that occurred to the Canadian crew of a de Havilland 9 day-bomber illustrates the dangers of the squadron's task.

The bombers were engaged in a low-level strafing attack against a large body of Red cavalry when a bullet disabled the engine of the plane piloted by a Lieutenant Elliot. He managed to bring the big two-seater down to a safe landing, only to face a line of charging Red cavalry. Elliot and his observer fought off the Red soldiers with twin Lewis guns in the rear cockpit. Meanwhile, another plane in the same formation noticed their danger and a second de Havilland, piloted by another Canadian, a Captain Anderson, circled to land, while the observer poured bullets from his Lewis guns into the mass of cavalry below.

Under the combined firepower of four Lewis guns, the Communist horsemen kept their distance. No doubt they thought it was only a matter of time until the machine guns ran out of ammunition. Stripping the guns from their crippled plane, Elliot and his observer dashed to Captain Anderson's aircraft, firing from the hip as they ran. They had just reached the plane when a Communist bullet punctured the gas tank of the rescue machine and gasoline gushed out through the hole.

Undaunted, Anderson's observer calmly climbed onto the lower wing and plugged the hole with a gloved thumb. Elliot and his companion leaped into the empty rear cockpit and Anderson hit the throttle. As the heavy-laden DH lunged forward the wildly shouting horsemen galloped after it, firing furiously as the plane gathered speed. Amid a hail of bullets, the DH lifted sluggishly from the ground. With its precious gas load saved by the resourceful observer, the plane returned safely to its base. The only "casualty" was the observer's thumb, which became temporarily paralyzed by its immersion in gasoline.

Rapid troop movements created some problems for the flyers, since there was always the possibility, when they returned from a flight, of finding their field in enemy hands. Collishaw related one such incident, when the field was encircled by Red cavalry after the White forces had retreated. The aircraft had to take off and hold back the Reds with machine guns and bombs until the ground crew could pack up and move out.

Beside the dangers of war, famine and disease stalked the land. Collishaw almost fell victim to the latter when, on a reconnaissance patrol in a de Havilland two-seater, his engine was damaged by ground fire and he was forced to land. With his observer, Collishaw had to walk six miles to the nearest railroad station to find transport back to the squadron. Aboard the crowded troop train, filled with verminous Russian peasants and soldiery, he fell ill. Back at Stalingrad, a doctor packed him off on a hospital train for evacuation from the front line. For five days Collishaw lay delirious and racked by deadly Typhus fever on a bunk in the baggage car of the train. Had it not been for the kindness of a refugee noblewoman he would have died. The train stopped for fuel and water at a small village, where an elderly Russian countess heard of the gravely ill British pilot. She had him carried to the small, one-room cottage where she had lived since fleeing the Revolution, and for six weeks, while Collishaw lay unconscious, she nursed him.

Although Collishaw survived the disease which killed more people than the battles of the Revolution, he needed further care. Finally, a British plane from his unit landed near the village. The pilot, hearing that a British flyer was lying ill nearby, sought Collishaw out and flew him back to his unit. "I was never able to thank the countess, who disappeared in the turmoil of the Revolution," said Collishaw.

He returned to battle in the winter of 1919, when the White Army had reached the zenith of its success against the Reds. But the tide of fortune changed when rumours spread through the country that the White Army would restore the Czar if it were victorious. The peasantry pledged their support to the Bolsheviks and the front collapsed.

The RAF unit was all but encircled, deep within the Caucasus, hundreds of miles from the sea. With the Don and Kuban Cossacks, the RAF units began to fight their way through the encirclement. While the squadron's baggage and ground personnel travelled in their own armoured train, the planes flew daily missions, blasting a hole through the Bolshevik forces with machine guns and bombs. The planes were forced to take off and land from the open steppes, which were, fortunately, frozen as hard as a concrete landing strip. As it was, each day at least one plane would fall victim to hard service; it would be stripped of usable parts and burned.

The retreat progressed at a snail's pace. The goal of the hard-pressed airmen was the Crimea, five hundred miles away over open country. They armed the train with machine gun turrets taken from scrapped aircraft, and the guns were often used to beat off the attacks of marauding Red cavalry. Fuel and water for the locomotive were another problem; Collishaw had to order armed parties into each village that was passed to commandeer what was necessary. And so they crept through southern Russia in the dead of winter, pursued relentlessly by a Red Army armoured train armed with a nine-inch gun.

Collishaw's train carried a number of Russian civilians, the families of White Army officers. These unfortunates, terrified of being captured by the Reds, had begged to be allowed to accompany the RAF unit in its break-out to the sea. To make matters worse, Typhus broke out among them. Every morning the cars of the train had to be searched and cleared of the bodies of the elderly men, women, and children who had succumbed to the dread fever.

They won through, though, and Collishaw led his haggard band into the safety of the Crimea, where the British and French armies and navies had established a strong base. Offensive operations against the Reds were being continued here, even while preparations were under way to evacuate the Allied Expeditionary Force from Russia, and it was here that Collishaw once more barely missed capture and death. Intensive ground fire from a strong body of Bolshevik cavalry damaged his engine while he was on a reconnaissance mission. While the plane would not remain in the air, Collishaw found on landing that the engine would still turn over. Over miles and miles of bumpy ground and frozen waterway, he taxied the plane all the way back to the base.

Through the first months of 1920, the RAF pilots continued the fight, but by March it was all over. The Bolshevik Revolution was triumphant and the British airmen sailed out of Sevastopol for Constantinople, then to Britain. For his service in Russia Collishaw was awarded three Czarist decorations and the Order of the British Empire.

On his return, Collishaw found plenty of opportunities for making use of his flying skill. British planes were now being used in place of troops to police the more remote parts of the Empire. Collishaw was first sent to Persia, a British protectorate threatened by an outbreak of tribal warfare and Bolshevik expansion across its borders. Collishaw commanded a squadron stationed at Kalvine, on the Caspian Sea, and the unit saw hard fighting against Communist irregulars raiding into Persia. His service to the Crown was again recognized: in the King's New Year's Honours List of 1921 he was gazetted a Commander of the British Empire. Later he led another squadron which helped put down a rebellion among the Arab tribes in Mesopotamia, after which he was appointed to the command of the Royal Navy's Fleet Air Arm, operating from the aircraft carrier HMS *Courageous*.

Up to this point, Raymond Collishaw had crowded the adventure of three lifetimes into one; but World War Two and the most important challenges of his life still lay before him.

The summer of 1940 was no better nor worse than any other, as far as the people of the tiny Libyan harbour town of Tobruk were concerned. They were well used to temperatures that climbed over 100 degrees. True, there was some added inconvenience. It was hard to find shelter from the burning sun when most of the habitable buildings had been taken over by an occupying army, but with Arabic fatalism they accepted their lot and moved their families to meaner quarters.

Thousands of Italian soldiers and airmen had turned this natural harbour on Africa's north coast into a sprawling military base, and to them the oppressive heat was almost a living thing that sapped them of their strength and will. Under the relentless sun many had lost the enthusiasm with which they had greeted Benito Mussolini's announcement that Italy would be united with Hitler's Germany against her former allies, France and England.

It, was on one typically blistering day that bemedalled Italian generals stared with astonishment into the sky, where a lone plane, bearing the red, white, and blue roundels of the RAF, swooped out of the sun to pass just above the rooftops of the fortified town. It was a solemn occasion: a military funeral for one of Italy's great soldiers. The Italians showed their displeasure at the impertinent Englishman as flak batteries erupted around the harbour and airfield. Steadily holding its course, the plane passed through the barrage and flew directly over the funeral cortege. From an open hatch, a small, brightly coloured object plummeted to the earth. Italian officers in full dress uniform dived into the dust to escape the bomb blast they were sure would follow. The object thumped onto the hardbaked earth and ...lay silent. The plane shot skyward, executing violent evasive action, and vanished towards Egypt.

On the ground, there was silence. Finally a general peered over the rim of a slit trench at the object in the middle of the airfield. He nudged his aide, a full colonel: "Go see what it is," he snapped.

"Si, signor generale," the colonel replied, and summoned his aide. "Capitano, the generale wants to know what was dropped," he ordered.

The captain beckoned to a sergeant : "Go find out what the Englishman dropped," he snarled at the wide-eyed noncom.

"Caporale," roared the sergeant, "examine the object dropped by the plane."

The corporal surveyed his machine gun crew : "Giuseppe, you heard the sergente. Go find out."

A disconsolate private loped reluctantly to the object and prodded it gingerly with the 'muzzle of his rifle. A word passed back up the chain of command. The Italian officers brushed sentimental tears from their eyes and smiled after the rapidly disappearing dot on the horizon. The object was a wreath of mourning, swathed in the traditional black banners and bearing the condolences of a legendary flyer, Air Commodore Raymond Collishaw, RAF, for the death of another gallant airman, Marshal Italo Balbo of the Italian Air Force. Marshal Balbo had been killed by mistake several days earlier when his plane had crossed the Italian anti-aircraft defences of Tobruk before giving the proper recognition signals. The plane was promptly shot down by his compatriots and the Marshal killed. The gallantry of Collishaw's gesture was fully appreciated by the Italians, even though Ray Collishaw's pilots were to blame for the quick trigger fingers of the Italian gunners. The Tobruk garrison had come to expect that any plane which came on them unannounced would bear the markings of an RAF aircraft.

From the beginning of the campaign in the Western Desert, when Italy first entered the war on Germany's side in June, 1940, Collishaw's pilots had seized the initiative in combat and held it, despite the vastly superior forces of the enemy. Mussolini's war was only a few hours old when the RAF had struck from Egypt. Bombers and fighter bombers under the Canadian's command flew on El Adem, the main Italian air base in Cyrenaica, a province of Libya. In the dawn attack the bombers caught Italian aircraft on the ground and riddled them with bullets and bombs. The runways were pitted with craters and the buildings smashed. Italian losses were disastrously heavy, for the raid struck the heart of the main concentration of Italian air power which was poised for a thrust into Egypt.

Collishaw, as the commander of 202 Group, had carefully watched the build-up of Axis forces in Cyrenaica. When the news arrived that Italy had declared war, it was only a matter of hours before operational orders for the sortie had gone out from the group's headquarters at Maaten Bagush. The raid on El Adem was a master stroke that robbed Italy, supposedly the aggressor, of the initiative from the beginning of the desert campaign. The attack was the culmination of the lessons in strategy that Collishaw had learned during his twenty-four years as a military flyer. At no time during his career, however, had he faced a situation as challenging as that presented by Italy's entry into the Second World War.

Collishaw's command was outnumbered almost two to one by the air strength Italy mustered in Cyrenaica. His group was part of the Middle East Command under Air Chief Marshal Sir Arthur Longmore. The command encompassed a total area of four and a half million square miles and included Egypt, the Sudan, Palestine, TransJordan, East Africa, Aden, Somaliland, Iraq and adjacent territories, Cyprus, Turkey, the Balkans (Yugoslavia, Rumania, Bulgaria, and Greece), the Mediterranean Sea, the Red Sea, and the Persian Gulf. The air defences for this vast area consisted of twenty-nine squadrons of 300 first line planes. This force had no auxiliary support, such as local industry for repairs, and supplies from England were scarce, for they were needed in the Battle of Britain. Half of those first line planes in the Middle East Command were based in Egypt, under Collishaw's direct command. The task of his force was to defend Egypt and the Suez Canal, and maintain communications through the Red Sea.

Although his planes were described as "first line," they were actually a collection of old fighters, bombers, and defenceless reconnaissance machines. But they were the best available throughout the Middle East Command. Collishaw persistently campaigned to give his pilots the most efficient equipment that could be had. Even so, his main bomber squadrons were equipped with vintage Blenheim 1 medium-range bombers or slow-moving Sunderland flying boats, while the five fighter squadrons at his disposal flew the antique Gloster Gladiator biplane. Other squadrons in the group were equipped with old warhorses such as the Fairey Battles, Hardys, Audaxes, Hawker Harts, Londons, and other types designed and built in the mid-1930's, a total of less than 200 aircraft.

Against these modest forces the Italians mustered a front line force of 479 planes: 282 based in Libya, 150 in Italian East Africa, and another 47 at the Dodecanese whence they could easily strike at Egypt. Behind this front line force were 1,200 more aircraft based on the Italian mainland, while strengthening Italy's hand further was a short supply line from Sicily, to provide repair and auxiliary forces to keep the front line force operational. For the Allies the situation was grim.

The Italian ground force, mainly infantry divisions but with some added motorized and armoured forces, was concentrated in Eastern Cyrenaica while its commander, Marshal Graziani, laid his plans for a rapid advance against the British in Egypt. His preparations were completed by midSeptember and the signal for the advance was given. Meanwhile, Collishaw had not been idle. Following the initial raid at El Adem, his Blenheims struck along the frontier against Italian ports, communications lines, and troop concentrations. The heavy Bombay bombers of his group thundered through the night to bomb Tobruk, while the highly vulnerable Lysanders of his reconnaissance squadrons ferreted out information about the forward positions of the enemy forces. The bombers achieved a notable success at Tobruk, scoring repeated hits on the Italian battle cruiser, the San Giorgio, which was burned out and beached. Fighter planes from Collishaw's group also provided air support for a naval raid on the staging areas and installations at Bardia. During the bombardment, the Gloster Gladiators shot down eight Italian fighters.

At the same time, Collishaw launched another attack against Italian airfields. Along the entire frontier, British planes "fumigated" the air bases, destroying Italian planes on the ground. At sea, fighters from the group provided air protection for the convoys to Malta and escorted Swordfish torpedo bombers in their attacks against Italian naval units and installations. Another success was recorded on August 15, when Collishaw's group attacked the seaplane base at Bomba, crippling twelve seaplanes. But the most successful and audacious attack was a raid on a heavily defended ammunition dump at Bardia. Successive blasts from burning ammunition rocked the bombers as they roared over the target and a huge shroud of smoke from the burning base was visible for miles.

The greatest achievement of Collishaw's aggressive policy was the instillation of a timid, defensive attitude into the enemy. As a result, the Italians managed to launch only a few attacks against such vulnerable British bases as Alexandria. Their only success of note was an air attack on Haifa, where several oil storage tanks were set afire. Collishaw recognized that operations such as he planned could not be carried out without casualties, and was prepared to accept the risk on the grounds that the end justified the means. On the other hand, it was only natural for his superiors to watch the casualty list instead of counting the number of British bases that escaped air raid because of Collishaw's attack strategy. The huge RAF repair depot at Aboukir was but one of the many juicy targets available for Italian bombers. Had the Italians regained the initiative, a series of blows at such installations could well have crippled, if not dismembered, the RAF in the Middle East. Collishaw's superiors must have overlooked this fact, for twice during this part of the campaign, Collishaw was rebuked for pressing the attacks far behind the enemy lines. "I consider such operations unjustified having regard to our limited resources, of which you are well aware," wrote Air Marshal Sir Arthur Longmore, Air Officer Commanding, from his headquarters in Cairo. Under his orders, reconnaissance flights were drastically reduced and bombing attacks against troop concentrations were forbidden for forces greater than one squadron.

The Italian attack, when it finally developed, was stopped cold by the British Eighth Army, under the command of Sir Archibald Wavell. With Egypt secure, the British themselves launched an attack that winter. Now the tethers were loosened, and Collishaw's aircraft worked in close support with the attacking army. The Canadian, still restricted by the lack of equipment, worked far into the night at his tented headquarters in the sandy wasteland near Mersa Matruh, devising methods to obtain the best possible results with the ancient aircraft at his disposal. One thing he had noted was the negligible effect that Italian aircraft had had on British tanks. Aerial machine gun fire just rattled off the tough hides of the armour-plated monsters. He therefore ordered his own planes to avoid attacks on tanks and instead to concentrate against the columns of trucks carrying gasoline and ammunition up to the front. Collishaw reasoned, correctly, that without these necessary supplies the Italian tanks would soon be forced to withdraw from the fight.

Another example of his ingenuity was the single Hurricane fighter that came to be known as "Collishaw's air force." As Italian aircraft losses mounted, Italy was forced to count on supplies from her German ally. Soon superior German types of aircraft, notably the Junkers 87 dive bomber and the ME-109 fighter, began to appear wearing Italian markings. To give the Italians the idea that his Desert Air Force was also being resupplied with improved aircraft, Collishaw made unorthodox use of a single Hurricane fighter. The plane had been sent to acquaint the pilots of the Desert Air Force with its features before large numbers of its type were dispatched. Collishaw used the single fighter as a propaganda weapon. He moved it from airfield to airfield, flying his single modern fighter close to Italian positions so that it could be recognized, and leaving the Italian air force with the impression that the fast new eight-gun fighters had arrived en masse in Libya. Pilots in the group quickly dubbed the plane "Collishaw's air force" and went out to battle again and again in their ancient Gladiators and Blenheims.

Another Collishaw innovation that played havoc with the enemy was a special impact bomb he devised for use against enemy airfields. The standard aerial bomb, he found, was unsuited for targets as widely dispersed as aircraft were when parked at their fields. It wasted much of its force digging a deep crater. Collishaw's new missile spread shrapnel over a wide area, thus damaging, if not destroying, planes parked a good distance from the impact point..

By the close of 1940 British arms, both on the ground and in the air, had won unqualified success. The Italians had been driven completely out of Cyrenaica and were in danger of losing even a toehold in North Africa. This was the period to which Hitler often referred when, later in the war, he said that England could have surrendered to Germany and still retained her honour because of her brilliant victories against the Italians. Despite odds that had increased to almost six to one, 1,200 Italian aircraft had been destroyed by Collishaw's air group. The entire Fifth Air Squadron of Mussolini's proud air force, the Regia Aeronautica, had been virtually obliterated. In addition, Wavell's ground forces had administered total defeat to the Italian Tenth Army and had captured most of the enemy's artillery and armour.

Then, on New Year's Day, 1941, the Luftwaffe arrived in the Mediterranean. The shipping route via Gibraltar was thus closed. There had been a redistribution of the RAF's Middle East air forces and 202 Group had been pulled out of Cyrenaica. Many of the Desert Air Force's experienced pilots and their planes had been sent to Crete, where they were lost. Some of its forces, redesignated 204 Group, had been moved into the former Italian territories, with several squadrons based at Tobruk itself. With the appearance of German fighters and bombers, and the imminent arrival of German ground forces, Collishaw renewed his appeals for newer and faster aircraft. But now, with Gibraltar sealed, the supply line from England was even longer, stretching around the African coast to Takoradi. Some of Collishaw's South African squadrons were equipped with Hurricanes, but the group was still far below the strength required to meet the new threat.

In the see-saw battles fought across the burning Libyan wastes, the tide had turned against the British once more. The lack of equipment made itself apparent when Wavell launched a strong attack against Sollum. He was hoping that the arrival of a Tiger convoy loaded with tanks and planes, the first to come through Gibraltar since the Luftwaffe had arrived, would offset losses in this attack. Collishaw's air group was called on to maintain a standing patrol over the attacking British ground forces. But because the group was underarmed the patrols were weak. As a result, the RAF lost three planes to the German one and the attack failed to achieve its main objectives.

It was at this time that Collishaw made a direct appeal to the Air Ministry in England for more planes and men. Indeed, they were on the way; but so were orders for a change in the command of both the air and ground forces. Collishaw had been unfairly criticized for his handling of the slim forces at his disposal. One war correspondent went so far as to describe him as an "individual style fighter who preferred spectacular tip and run raids to the concerted bombing attacks on enemy forces which were necessary for Wavell's success ... [His replacement,] Air Vice-Marshal Arthur Coningham, had none of Collishaw's *drawbacks.*" This despite the heavy losses at Sollum which should have demonstrated that Collishaw's forces were far too slim for such "concerted bombing attacks."

The desert campaign was one fraught with very special hardships. The heat, sand, dust, and lack of water destroyed both men and machines. Engines overheated and burned themselves out, gears became choked with sand and were crippled, tanks and aircraft had to be specially serviced for desert work. On men, the desert was equally harsh. For the better part of a year, working day and night, enduring the same conditions as the least of the men in his command, Collishaw had fought a successful battle against superior odds only to find a fresh, better-equipped enemy opposing him on the road to victory. Though exhausted, he was still ready to continue the fight with the fresh men and machines which were at last arriving, but his orders were explicit. He turned over his command to Coningham and left the front. On returning to Britain, he commanded a fighter group for the better part of a year.

In 1943, buried on an inside page, a Toronto paper carried the story of Collishaw's retirement from the RAF. In a reprint of an article from the *London Gazette, The Globe and Mail* gave Collishaw's age as forty-eight and stated that he was among the first six most successful pilots of the First War, only outranked among the Canadians by Bishop and Barker. The brevity of the story and its secluded spot deep within the pages of the newspaper probably suited the publicity-shy Raymond Collishaw perfectly. On leaving the service he returned to Canada and moved to British Columbia, where he now lives.

Slowly, and with great difficulty, heavily armed convoys fought through to win the battle of supply in North Africa for the Allies. More and more planes, tanks, guns, and men were pumped into the Western Desert to build up a strong force that, after bitter fighting, defeated the Afrika Korps of Field Marshal Rommel at El Alamein. Among the victorious forces were the survivors of Ray Collishaw's Desert Air Force who had gathered in the tented headquarters at Maaten Bagush a year earlier to hear the Canadian commander outline his attack philosophy. They had learned their profession under this master flyer, and they in turn had passed on their knowledge to the new pilots who played such a vital role in the Allied triumph. Thus Air Vice Marshal Raymond Collishaw contributed to the German defeat, even in his absence.

Black Mike

When Bill Barker was transferred in 1918, "Black Mike" McEwen became the top ace of No. 28 Squadron in Italy. Although his list of victories never reached the proportions of Bishop's or Barker's, McEwen was no ordinary flyer. Like so many of the young Canadians in the air, he possessed a boldness that expressed itself in experimentation and innovation. Newcomers to the business of war, the Canadians willingly accepted the commands and advice of their more experienced European contemporaries. Nevertheless, they worked for the day when they would run their own show. While they learned the fundamentals of military science from their seniors, Canadians brought fresh ideas to combat flying.

Born in Griswold, Manitoba, McEwen was a graduate of Moose Jaw College and the University of Saskatchewan. He enlisted in the Canadian Army in March, 1916, and transferred to the RFC in June, 1917. He graduated from the flying school at Reading as a qualified Camel pilot just in time to join 28 Squadron when it left England for active service in France. The sinister nickname of "Black Mike" was given McEwen while training at Camp Borden. Its origin was quite innocent. "I tan fairly easily—and it was a hot summer," he explained.

McEwen went on his first war patrol on November 29, 1917, as a member of Barker's C Flight. On February 18, McEwen shot down the fifth enemy aircraft required to qualify for the coveted title of ace. The battle took place at 15,000 feet over the town of Rustigno. "While on offensive patrol," McEwen wrote in his combat report, "my engine began to run badly. I left the patrol and flew back towards the lines, heading southeast. My engine picked up and on recrossing the lines to rejoin the patrol, I sighted an e.a. [enemy aircraft] below me. I got in several bursts and the e. a. did not offer to avoid me and went down out of control. As my goggles frosted up I could only follow him down to 4,000 feet. I last saw him out of control over Rustigno...."

The frosted goggles, which forced McEwen to pull up to avoid flying blind into the side of a mountain, robbed him of official confirmation. It was not until some time later that the wreckage of the plane was found and he was given credit for the victory.

When Barker left 28 Squadron, C Flight found itself with a new commander. The replacement was Captain Stan Stanger of Montreal. In Stanger, McEwen found a companion as well as a commander, and it was not long before the two were wingmates, flying on many combat missions together. As a team they were hard to beat.

On the morning of May 2, 1918, Stanger and McEwen took off for an offensive patrol over the Austrian lines. Their mission was to destroy enemy reconnaissance planes which had been prowling the Allied positions. They were looking for trouble and soon found it over the town of Valdobbiadene. Beneath their wings, ten of the new, more powerful Albatros D-5's huddled protectively around the bulkier shape of an Aviatik observation plane. Without hesitation the two Canadians pushed their control sticks forward and the noses of the Camels dropped into a dive. The two planes separated as they neared the Austrian formation, with McEwen acting the part of decoy to try and lure the fighter escort into battle, while Stanger went after the two-seater. But the pilot of the reconnaissance plane would not play their game and dropped out of the formation, pushing the nose of his plane down to gain speed and streaking for home.

As a result the two Canadians found themselves in the midst of a hornet's nest of Austrian fighters; the Austrians had broken off in all directions, manoeuvring violently in an attempt to get a shot at the British planes. For five minutes the two Canadians fought their ten adversaries. Then Stanger saw the cautious Aviatik peep out of a cloud. Ignoring the encircling fighters, he sent his plane racing after the two-seater. This was the principal quarry, for the pictures of ground positions taken by observation planes often cost the lives of thousands of men. Stanger was determined that this plane would not get back to Austrian headquarters with its vital information. So while McEwen tried to keep the ten enemy fighters occupied, Stanger streaked after the Aviatik. Too late the Austrian pilot saw his danger. Angling in from the side, Stanger's bullets raked the two-seater from tail fin to propeller and the plane rolled lazily onto its back and careened to the earth. From high above, Stanger watched it explode on the ground, then turned his plane back to help his companion.

McEwen, in the meantime, had his hands full trying to avoid the concentrated fire of twenty machine guns. Seeing Stanger returning, he dropped his defensive tactics and attacked. Tracers from his guns smashed into the motor and gas tank of the closest Albatros and the plane went into a dive, trailing smoke and fire. The fight had lasted ten minutes now, and Stanger's guns had already clicked on empty chambers. McEwen was not much better off, for only a few rounds remained in the belts of his guns. They had achieved their purpose in the destruction of the enemy observation plane. There was nothing more that could be accomplished with empty guns, so they made for the deck and headed home, successfully eluding the Austrians.

In those early days of aerial warfare, "close support" was just that: a group of fighters would be tacked to a bomber formation with orders to attack any marauding enemy fighters that came too close. These tactics were purely defensive and robbed the escorting planes of the initiative which is essential for successful fighter operations. It was through hard experience that McEwen and some fellow pilots recognized the definite disadvantage of these tactics.

They had learned that fighter planes on escort mission should anticipate trouble and go out and meet it. If the fighters were bound to the close escort system, enemy formations stacked high in the clouds could fight a battle of their own choosing, waiting for reinforcements to arrive and attacking only when the moment suited them. One way to prevent this was to give the fighter escort sufficient freedom in its assignment so that a portion of the fighters could be detached to break up the enemy formations before they could launch their attack.

An effective demonstration of this theory was staged by McEwen on June 19, 1918. McEwen and two other pilots had been assigned to protect two Bristol fighters on a reconnaissance patrol. The group was over the Austrian lines at 15,000 feet when McEwen spotted six enemy fighters—fast new Berg Scouts—coming in on the Bristols from astern. Apparently the only other man to spot the approaching enemy fighters was the observer of the rearmost Bristol, for he fired a warning flare. The signal was lost to all but McEwen, who put his plane into a wingover and turned back to meet the Bergs. They were now roaring in on the trailing Bristol, firing steadily, but with no results. Having missed in their first pass, and thinking themselves undiscovered, the Bergs wheeled away, no doubt planning to reform and ambush the flight later from a convenient cloudbank.

If this was their plan they never had a chance to realize it. McEwen was in hot pursuit. He opened fire from long range, and the enemy pilots, looking back, discovered only one of the Canadians behind them. It was probably at the same moment that McEwen realized he was alone. His companions, unaware of the attack of the Austrian fighters, had continued on their way, and the Canadian, now separated from his formation, found himself surrounded by six angry Austrian flyers.

McEwen decided the best defence was to attack. He promptly sent a burst of machine gun bullets into the nearest Berg, which took fire and plunged towards the earth. With one enemy plane flaming, McEwen attacked another and drove it down in an out-of-control spin. Now the remaining four, with the advantage of height, launched a determined attack against the Camel. With no help in sight, McEwen dived for the cover of the ground. In his extremity the peculiar advantages of the little Camel came to his aid. At low altitude he headed his plane into the narrow Astico Valley, a small opening in the mountains. The enemy fighters followed him for some distance along the twisting course, but as the hills rose higher and higher on each side of the five planes the clumsier Austrians were forced to gain altitude to avoid the hillsides and had to allow the nimble Camel, to escape.

McEwen's action in taking the initiative and attacking the attackers had destroyed the Austrians' advantage and had enabled the two-seaters to carry out their mission. In the months that followed, this policy became standard procedure, with the scouts ranging the skies far above and in front of the two-seaters and breaking up concentrations of enemy fighters before they could launch their attack against the prime target. In the Second World War, McEwen's lesson was forgotten for a while. Fighters were again saddled with close escort roles on missions with bombers and the lesson had to be learned all over again.

It was during June that McEwen was awarded the Distinguished Flying Cross. He was now considered one of 28 Squadron's brightest stars. In recommending McEwen for a citation, the squadron commander, Major Claude Ridley, said of the Canadian: "... an excellent pilot ... conspicuous for his dash and fighting judgement, both in combat and on the low bombing raids carried out by his squadron. On one of two raids in which he took part, his machine was riddled with bullets and his petrol tank pierced by heavy tracer fire, but he succeeded in returning to his aerodrome. He is one of the keenest and most reliable pilots in the squadron."

Combined with Stanger, McEwen, also made up the most successful team of 28 Squadron. On October 4, 1918, the two men were paired up as an escort for a bombing raid by two squadrons on the Austrian aerodrome at Campoformido. It would be a long-range operation, through country heavily patrolled by enemy fighters. For this reason fighters had been chosen for the bombing mission because it was felt that they would have the speed necessary to achieve surprise and, after unloading their bombs, would be able to fight their way back to their own lines. It was an ambitious plan for those days, with loads calling for forty-pound phosphorous bombs besides the twenty-five pounders usually carried by Camels. Number 28 Squadron supplied twelve planes for the raid, while 66 Squadron sent eleven more.

Since the fighters would be laden beyond their normal capacity on the run in to the target, it was decided to provide them with an escort. McEwen and

Stanger were given the job of flying top cover over the attack force. The twenty-three-plane formation hugged the ground on the way to the target, meeting only occasional anti-aircraft fire as the Austrian army was now in full retreat. The achievement of total surprise seemed to be theirs, when suddenly McEwen and Stanger spotted six Albatros D-5's moving in to intercept the heavily laden formation. With their speedier ships, the enemy pilots would have a decided advantage over the bomb-carrying Camels, who would either have to suffer the attack or jettison their bomb loads into the empty fields below in order to resist.

There was no time for hesitation, and, despite the uneven odds, both McEwen and Stanger pushed their sticks forward, diving on the enemy flight with motors roaring full out. They dropped like stones on the tail of the Austrian formation. Each picked a target and opened fire at close range. Stanger's garishly painted opponent fell off on one wing under the hail of machine gun fire and went into an uncontrolled dive. Seconds later McEwen's foe went into a spin and crashed near the first victim. Thoroughly disorganized, the Austrian formation broke off wildly and banked for home and safety, with the two Canadians in hot pursuit. Stanger opened fire on one from long range and watched his tracers lacing the air around the weaving, dodging Albatros. Pieces of the machine suddenly broke away into the slip-stream as the machine gun fire took effect and a third black-crossed fighter splashed into the marshes of the Tagliamento River. McEwen, meanwhile, was chasing the remaining three, but their more powerful motors soon pulled them away from his Camel.

In high spirits the two Canadians rejoined the bomber formation, which carried out its attack on ground targets with "excellent results." The mission had generated a brilliant defensive action which was a fitting finale for McEwen's career, for the following day 28 Squadron conducted its last battle operation on the Italian front, and on November 4 Austria sued for peace.

In the eleven months between October 20, 1917, and November 4, 1918, 28 Squadron had destroyed 111 enemy, aircraft, driven down another 25 out of control, and dropped a total of 23,400 pounds of bombs. Its pilots had won one Distinguished Service Order, four Military Crosses, one bar to the MC, five Distinguished Flying Crosses, one bar to the DFC, and eight Italian decorations. Of these twenty awards, ten went to Canadian pilots. In these last days of the war McEwen was promoted to captain and put in command of his own flight. At the time of the Armistice he was 28 Squadron's top-scoring ace.

On November 11, 1918, just a week after the collapse of Austria, Germany asked for terms and the war ended. From Switzerland to the North Sea the guns fell silent. Men cautiously stood up in their muddy trenches and stared at the enemy across the forbidding stretch of barbed wire and shell craters which was no man's land. Four years of hatred and slaughter had decimated an entire generation. The survivors, skilled at trench raids and bayonet fighting, uneasily contemplated a future for which they were totally unprepared. Boys had grown to manhood in combat and the years usually spent learning a trade or profession had vanished in the fire of war.

Whilst aviation had proven itself during the war, all but a few visionaries failed to see how airplanes could be of use in a world of peace. It was up to the same men who had fought in the air to win for their branch of the military a status separate from the Army and Navy. Some of them began to undertake another lengthy battle: to convince the sceptics that flying was more than just a spectacular wartime innovation. Thousands of flyers had graduated from the flying schools of England and Canada during the war, but with the peace they found themselves unemployed. The business world had failed to recognize the tremendous potential of the airplane as a means of exploration and of rapid transportation of goods and passengers, while the general public tended to regard flying as a risky form of sport.

Despite such ignorance and apathy Canada did have airplanes. At the end of the war the British Government had presented Canada with a gift of one hundred machines with which to start the Canadian Air Force. The first squadron of the force was presented with its colours at a special ceremony at Buckingham Palace shortly after the Armistice. The Canadian Air Force was the brainchild of an imposing list of experts, who held, senior jobs in the new service. They included Billy Bishop, Don MacLaren and Black Mike McEwen.

With their fleet of war-weary battle planes, these men set out to prove to Canada that the airplane could play a significant role in the development of the country. It was no easy task, for there was great public opposition to the idea of maintaining a permanent peacetime air force. The people of Canada were tired of high wartime costs and the government was reluctant to spend any money to build up the Air Force.

Some pilots tried to prove the airplane's peacetime potential on their own. They bought surplus war planes and barnstormed the country, doing tricks and aerobatics , at county fairs, taking passengers up for a dollar a ride, or delivering small cargoes for business concerns. Others realized that only the Air Force could provide the machines and material necessary to further the progress of flying in Canada. They elected to remain in the service. Among them was Black Mike.

There was no lack of work to be done. The Air Force set out to adapt the old two-seater Bristols and de Havillands to peacetime use. The planes that had once photographed enemy entrenchments and artillery batteries now flew long missions into the remote Canadian north, taking photographs for surveys and mapmaking, carrying supplies to government and RCMP posts, and researching new methods of air freighting, navigation, and flight procedure. It was hard, often dangerous, work. It is to the credit of these men that every airline route now used in Canada was pioneered by early RCAF pilots.

In the latter half of the 1930's, war clouds once more began to gather in Europe, however. Work was begun to refurbish and rearm the RCAF. One of the major projects during this period was the construction of a huge training base at Trenton, Ontario. It immediately became one of the focal points for a vast air training plan and it was here that McEwen was stationed when the Second World War began.

From Trenton he was appointed commanding officer of a Coastal Command group based in Newfoundland, where the war against the submarine menace was a twenty-fourhour job. The long, dangerous patrols over the vast expanse of the North Atlantic played a significant role in breaking up the submarine wolf packs. The U-boats were forced to operate in mid-ocean to avoid the far-ranging planes of McEwen's group.

Meanwhile fate was shaping a different course for the former fighter pilot. In the First World War a squadron commander had said of McEwen: "He has done much to stimulate the enthusiasm essential to good work among the junior officers." This ability to "stimulate the enthusiasm" of young flyers now led him to the command of one of the most successful bomber groups in the Second World War.

When the war began in 1939, the Canadian Government had advanced strong arguments for maintaining the identity of Canadian forces. In the First War there had been no Canadian air force, and Canadian pilots had served with British squadrons. Now Canada wanted the new RCAF to maintain its autonomy, rather than have individual Canadians, or even entire RCAF squadrons, integrated into existing RAF units. In 1943 that goal was realized with the creation of Six Group, an all-Canadian bomber group that was to become the showpiece of the RCAF. Its performance in the field of heavy bombardment was unexcelled.

The opposition to RCAF autonomy was partly based on the fallacy that while Canadians were first class pilots, they lacked the military know-how needed by top-level tacticians. This opinion may have had its origin in the brilliant but often unorthodox combat records of Canadian flyers in the First Great War. Could such wild fighter pilots now undertake the precise and intricate business of mounting and carrying out long-range bombing attacks? The young Canadian airmen of the forties had to prove that the answer was Yes. Men whose fathers had created the legend of the daring and madcap pursuit pilot now had to create a new image, that of the cool, steady flyer who could take a multiengine heavy bomber in tight formation through a storm of flak and unload his bombs on target.

Although Six Group became operational on New Year's Day, 1943, it was a bomber group in name only, since most of the Canadian squadrons overseas were still under the command of the RAF's Four Bomber Group. At the outset the group consisted of eight squadrons equipped with Wellington and Halifax bombers. By the end of the war six more squadrons had been added, flying the improved Halifax bomber and the Canadian-built Lancaster. The group's aircraft were originally serviced by RAF personnel, but these were gradually replaced by Canadians, and, by 1945, the group was almost one hundred per cent Canadian.

Heavy bombardment, more than any other type of aerial combat operation, is a team effort, one that relies heavily on the ability and experience of the coach who is calling the plays. As in any group activity, morale and efficiency usually go hand in hand, and they are invariably products of great leadership. Six Group had that leadership.

On February 29, 1944, a straight-shouldered, athletic looking officer, his upper lip adorned with a bristling black moustache, pushed through the doors of Allerton Hall, an ancient manor house in Yorkshire, and presented his credentials to the sergeant on duty. The sergeant checked the papers, noted the broad stripe of an air commodore on the visitor's sleeve, and sprang to attention. "This way, sir, we've been expecting you," he said, leading the way through cluttered offices to a door bearing the legend: "Air Officer Commanding."

Behind them, office workers paused over their typewriters and filing cabinets to straighten their ties or check that all the buttons of their tunics were fastened. "Smarten up," whispered one to a companion. "That's the new AOC and he's a stickler for proper dress."

Black Mike McEwen had been overseas for more than a year as a station commander when he was given orders to take over as commanding officer for the entire Six Group. When he was first posted overseas from his Coastal Command job in Newfoundland he had hoped to lead one of the new fighter-intruder wings of the Tactical Air Force which had been formed after the Battle of Britain. Now he threw all his energy into his new command, for although his first love would always be the fighter plane, he recognized the equally important role of the heavies.

Allerton Hall, the ancient building that served as McEwen's headquarters, was steeped in history, but to the men of Six Group it was always known as

"Castle Dismal." from this building came the operational orders for the RCAF'S largest overseas formation. Now a new signature appeared on those orders, and a new personality made itself felt. Black Mike was determined that his command, while remaining distinctively Canadian, should rival the most disciplined unit in action.

One of his first moves on taking command was to order a full-scale programme of flight training. For air crews who were already veterans of operations over enemy territory, this came as a surprise. Six Group had its own peculiar problems, however. Its flying fields were the most northern of any group in Bomber Command and therefore the most distant from the targets on the Continent. This meant that, on the average, Canadian air crews were in the air longer than the crews from other groups. Moreover, the Vale of York was difficult country for flying. Because most of the country was formed of rolling hills, Six Group's airfields were located close together. Thus landing circuits sometimes overlapped. Smog from nearby industrial complexes, combining with the low clouds that persisted in the area, tended to increase the already considerable hazards of bringing in big bombers for night landings after a mission. While air crews grumbled about the training programme instituted by McEwen, experts later credited the programme with the group's successes and low casualty rate.

Six Group also found that their new CO was no swivelchair commander. Although there was a superstition among air crew against brass riding in bombers during ops, McEwen's presence in the bomber force was soon taken for granted, and he even became a good luck symbol. As the men saw it, when the "man with the moustache" was along, things were going to be fine. Men always respond to a leader who shows concern for their welfare. They felt drawn to this colourful airman who wanted to share the dangers with them, and who, when finally ordered to stay on the ground, could not sleep when his men were away on a raid.

McEwen's influence changed another well-entrenched air crew custom. This was the "fifty mission" look, a sartorial quirk cultivated by many airmen. It grew from the informal, and sometimes downright sloppy, attire adopted by fighter pilots early in the war. At that time there was some excuse for it, for during the Battle of Britain fighter pilots engaged on six to ten sorties a day had little time for polished brass and creased trousers. But as the war progressed and the pressure eased, the fad continued. The American air force quickly snapped up the style of floppy hats and tarnished brass as a means of proving themselves old hands at the business of combat flying.

The fad was widespread, but the style had a cold reception in Six Group. McEwen put out an order requiring all officers to dress as officers, and non-commissioned ranks, whether air or ground crew, to be properly and neatly attired. As a result, Six Group personnel were band-box trim in their dress, a fact unusual enough to rate a mention in a Time magazine feature story about the group in October, 1944. "They scorn casual attire," the correspondent wrote. "The wire is in their caps ... and they appear ready for a dress parade... men of all squadrons [in the group] consider themselves the cream of the RCAF."

It was good psychology, since pride in appearance is one of the basic steps towards creating that nebulous quality called team spirit. Six Group men felt that they had no need to wear the costume of combat veterans; they knew that they had carried their share of the terrifying burden of the air offensive, and that knowledge was sufficient. They were "Black Mike's Boys" and proud of it.

McEwen assumed command of Six Group at a critical juncture in the air war. Although the tide of the global conflict had turned in favour of the Allies, German fighter production had reached an all-time high, and the bomber formations attacking Germany's war industries were suffering staggering losses. Bomber attacks had originally been considered nothing more than nuisance raids by many highly placed political figures early in the war. At that time the value of bombing raids was doubtful, because of primitive equipment and tactics and the necessity for clear weather if the target was even to be reached, let alone bombed successfully. However, by 1943 and 1944 radar aids known as "H2S" and "Oboe" had been developed to guide the big bomber fleets into Germany and enable them to "see" a target even though it was obscured by clouds.

At the same time German radar had also improved, which meant that the attacks on bomber formations by the Luftwaffe's fighters became more accurate. Nevertheless, round-the-clock bombing continued ceaselessly. There was a popular song at the time, repeated endlessly on radio programmes, "The USA by Day and the RAF by Night" and, as in the song, tight formations of American Flying Fortresses and Liberators of the Eighth Air Force pushed deeper and deeper into Germany against stiffening fighter resistance, while at night RAF and RCAF Lancasters, Wellingtons, Halifaxes, and Stirlings experimented with their new bomber stream tactics over the prime targets in Hitler's Reich.

This was the Battle of the Ruhr, and the pilots of the battle sang an equally light-hearted song, an adaptation of an old military favourite, "The Quartermaster's Stores." In the pubs and mess halls the air gunners and pilots raised their voices lustily, bellowing lyrics that contained an ominous meaning: "O there's flak, flak, all that you can pack, in the Valley of the Ruhr."

Back from night raids over Germany, haggard bomber pilots told intelligence officers: "The flak was so thick you could walk on it." "Jerry's got a new night fighter; we lost two planes before we knew what hit us." "We were coned by the searchlights and the fighters and flak did the rest." "We hit the primary target through nine-tenths cloud cover; it burned like a volcano."

Night after night the quiet hills of Yorkshire, the Midlands, and Devonshire trembled under the blast of heavy motors as the giant, four-engined bombers lumbered off the ground like torpid, airborne whales and headed for the black, menacing ocean of sky over the Continent, an ocean prowled by the shark-like night fighters of the Luftwaffe. Day after day, the communiques informed the people of the world: "Last night aircraft from Bomber Command were operating over Lorient ... or Essen ... or Hamburg ... or Berlin." Sometimes the communiques ended with the cryptic message: "Five of our aircraft are missing ... six of our aircraft ... ten."

Undated photo shows a Royal Air Force Handley Page model H.P. 59 Halifax B Mk. II Series 1A heavy bomber, coded EY*B, of No. 78 (Bomber) Squadron, No. 4 Group, Bomber Command, in flight. The B Mk. II prototype first flew July 3, 1941, with the first production model taking wing in September. The Series IA brought a 10 per cent improvement in performance to the slightly underpowered "heavy" -- particularly when fully loaded -- by cutting drag and weight. Changes included eliminating the forward turret in favour of a streamlined, Perspex nose, installing a lower-profile dorsal turret and further streamlining the engine nacelles, which housed uprated Rolls-Royce Merlin 22s or 24s. Late in the production run, the triangular fins were replaced by rectangular models to eliminate a deadly rudder stall condition; this feature became standard on subsequent marks.
Department of Natrional Defence/PL-116961

One night the target was Nuremberg and ninety-four bombers failed to return, thirteen of them crewed by Canadians. Conditions were perfect for the enemy fighters. A full moon silhouetted the bombers against the low lying cloud cover. Enemy ground controllers ignored a formation of 50 Halifaxes laying mines over the North Sea, a diversion that usually would have drawn away some of the fighter force. This time, stormy conditions over the water kept fighters close to home. The first intercepts developed east of Aachen and continued with mounting fury when the bomber stream swung south on the final leg of its journey to the target. "Free lance" night fighters were fed into the battle in ever increasing numbers. After the war, a German officer said that when daylight came, it was possible to chart the course of the bomber formation from the wrecked bombers on the ground: "They ran in a smouldering line across half of Germany."

The intensity of the German attacks is demonstrated by the experience of two Canadian aircraft. One survived the raid and one did not.

A Halifax from 424 "Tiger" Squadron, captained by Flying Officer F. F. Hamilton, was savagely mauled by a fighter's cannon and machine gun fire. Left with one engine burning and some of its controls shot away, the plane lost considerable altitude before the pilot regained control. But now the runaway propeller of the damaged engine threatened to shake the big plane to pieces. Attempts to feather the prop were unavailing until the situation remedied itself and the propeller flew off of its own accord. On its way home to base the Canadian plane was attacked twice more, but each time accurate fire from the crippled bomber's gunners drove the German planes away. Flying Officer Hamilton was awarded the DFC for this mission.

Another Halifax, from 429 "Bison" Squadron, was not so lucky. Set afire by an enemy fighter on its way to the target, its pilot, Flying Officer J. H. Wilson, maintained his course while his flight engineer, Sergeant Harry Glass, attacked the fire in the fuselage with extinguishers. Although the flames were quelled, the damage was too great for the plane to stay in the air. On the homeward flight, Flying Officer Wilson was forced to ditch the craft in the North Sea. The landing was a good one, but the plane was sinking fast, and two wounded crew members would have lost their lives but for Sergeant Glass, who helped them to the safety of the plane's rubber dinghy. (Sergeant Glass was awarded the Distinguished Flying Medal for that mission. In August, 1944, Glass, now a Flying Officer, was involved in another forced landing at sea. This time he was aboard a plane that had taken part in a massive Canadian attack on oil storage depots in the Foret de Chantilly. Badly damaged in the raid, the plane ditched in the English Channel. Six of the seven man crew were lost, and Flying Officer Glass was one of them.)

The Nuremberg attack dealt Six Group and Bomber Command one of its most severe blows. In a few short hours, close to one thousand trained airmen were killed or captured, and this was just one night in a battle that lasted more than a year.

Sometimes the bombers flew low, so that their time over target would be lessened and they would have more chance to avoid the batteries of heavy flak from the 88-, 90-, and 100-millimetre guns that ripped the curtain of night with hideous splashes of fire. Another time they would bomb from extreme altitude. This way they avoided the hosepipe stream of cannon shells from the multi-barrelled 20- and 40-millimetre light flak. Either way, casualties continued to mount.

Then there were the night fighters to contend with. First came the primitive "wild boar" tactics of a certain Major Hermann of the Luftwaffe: single engine fighters, ME-109's and Focke-Wulf 190's, lurked near heavy concentrations of searchlights, waiting for the lights to cone a hapless Wellington or Lancaster in their beams. The tactics were crude, and in the long run unsuccessful, but they seemed more than adequate to the sweating pilot of an RCAF bomber who fought to hold his burning plane in the air until his crew could bale out.

Later came the twin-engine ME-110's, the JU-88's, and the ME-410's: proper night fighters, with their noses bristling with radar antennae that found their prey and guided the bomber-destroyer to its quarry. As the war dragged on and the casualties continued to mount, the light-hearted songs about the "Valley of the Ruhr" and "The USA by Day" echoed hollowly in the ears of the survivors of so many hard-fought missions. Night after night the heavy-laden bombers swung aloft, and pilots strained their eyes into the inky blackness to find the landmarks that would guide them to their blacked-out targets, or watched the horizon for that familiar reddish glow on the bottom of the cloud cover that told them the Pathfinders had been in to mark the target.

"Fighters at three o'clock level. . . ." "Close up, you guys, come on, close up!" "Watch that brute, Harry, he's under your tail." "I got one ... he's flaming." "What are they?" " ... dunno, must be those new jets, they're plenty fast!"

It was late in the afternoon of March 31, 1945, and planes from Six Group were part of the bomber stream high over the shattered wreckage that had once been Hamburg. From the smoky skies, a gaggle of thirty of the 500-mile-an-hour Messerschmitt 262 jet fighters had jumped the Canadian bombers. With dramatic suddenness the twin-engine fighters had swept through the formation of heavy bombers, barely giving the gunners time to clear their guns with preliminary bursts before the action was joined. A Lancaster suddenly blossomed flame from a port engine and went into a shallow dive. Immediately a shark-nosed jet closed in on the cripple and cannon shells exploded along the bomber's fuselage and wings. The dive steepened and tiny figures leaped from the burning plane.

Over their intercoms, gunners swapped battle reports "Here's another one coming in ... at twelve o'clock level ... watch him, Bill, he'll roll over and you can get a shot at him as he passes our tail." The jets were handled with deadly skill, for these pilots were the cream of the German Luftwaffe, most of them holders of the Knight's Cross of the Iron Cross, Germany's highest award for bravery. The Canadian gunners hit back with their heavy machine guns, trying desperately to track the speedy jets with their guns. The last formation of Lancasters had arrived over the target ten minutes late and, without the fighter cover that had protected the earlier bombers that day, was paying the penalty for its tardiness. Expertly directed by ground controllers, the jets swarmed over the bombers, hoping for an easy victory. But the slower Lancasters were putting up a stiff fight. A jet suddenly exploded and the bombers flew right through the ball of flame. Another Messerschmitt rolled on its back, shed a wing under the heavy battering of a Lancaster's nose turret guns, and fell into a dive. The Canadians lost eight aircraft, but combat reports indicated that four of the new 262's had been destroyed, besides three probables, and three damaged.

At Castle Dismal, McEwen had watched his command grow from just over half a dozen squadrons equipped with twin-engine medium bombers to a force of fifteen squadrons equipped with the latest four-motor planes, each capable of fighting its way to the farthest enemy target and back. His rigid demand for operational training and flight discipline had paid valuable dividends, for while the number of sorties and planes had doubled since the group's first year of operations, losses had dropped. In 1943, the year of the furious air battles over Berlin, Six Group bombers had made 6,200 sorties into German territory.

During 1944, Black Mike and his boys had demonstrated their versatility by the variety of the tasks the group had carried out. The Canadian formation had taken on the dangerous assignment of dropping mines in Germany's inland waterways. These "gardening" operations, carried out in conjunction with the Group's commitment to the bombing offensive and utilizing small formations or even individual planes, destroyed or damaged large numbers of oceangoing Axis vessels in Germany's home waters. At the same time they were given the task of disrupting all rail communications in France just after the D-Day landings by Allied ground forces, while still carrying out their regular assignment of pattern bombing of German industrial centres. On July 28 the group had suffered its greatest loss when 209 aircraft were assigned to drop 903 tons of bombs on Hamburg. Over the target, the bombers met heavy concentrations of flak and searchlights. On the trip home, riding above a heavy cloud cover, they were hit by successive waves of German night fighters. Twenty-two Canadian bombers were lost that night, and the lights burned long into the grey dawn at Castle Dismal as senior staff officers sifted through the combat reports. That year the group recorded its total losses as 377 bombers. Actually, with experience and training, the group's loss ratio had been cut and the group had flown three times as many missions.

In the latter part of 1944 the heavy bombers were aided significantly by the establishment of radar and navigational stations in parts of France recaptured from the Germans by the Allied armies. These installations helped to guide the huge formations through the heaviest weather to and from their targets. The bombardment from the air had also disrupted the interception system of the German Fighter Control, while the increased range of fighter escorts "little friends," as they were known by the bomber crews and the work of Mosquito intruder squadrons had further reduced the effectiveness of Germany's fighter defences.

With Germany crumbling around him, Hitler decreed a glorious finale for his Third Reich. The evil genius who had tried to revive the cult of the ancient Teutonic gods stole a page from German folklore for the final rites of defeat. Just as the gods of Valhalla had commemorated their end with a ritual of fire and destruction—the "Twilight of the Gods"—so the Fuehrer proclaimed a Gotterddmmerung for his Nazi régime. With desperate fury, German fighter pilots hurled themselves at the Allied bomber fleets, and the new, long awaited secret weapons, the ME-262 jets, the Heinkel 162 Volksjadger (People's Fighter) rocket planes and the tiny, volatile Messerschmitt Komets joined the conventional FW-190's and ME-109's in the fight. But the new planes came too late. Had they been introduced a year earlier, when Germany's industries were still relatively intact, they might well have spelled the defeat of the Allied bomber offensive by inflicting unbearable losses on the British, Canadian, and American heavies. But as the year 1945 opened, the constant hammering at Germany's war industries had done its work.

By May, 1945, Six Group had won 2,230 awards for gallantry, including the two highest decorations in the British Empire, the George Cross and the Victoria Cross. The flyers joked about their "gongs" but their pride in their unit was immense. The last raid carried out by the Canadians was on April 25, 1945, when 184 bombers smashed the German coastal defence guns on Wangerooge Island to pave the way for Canadian and British ground assault forces. Although the Canadians were alerted for operations several times, the German collapse came swiftly. On May 8, Six Group celebrated with the rest of the world the end of the war in Europe.

Eight squadrons of the group, under the leadership of Black Mike, were earmarked for further combat duty in the Pacific, but this special "Tiger Force" was disbanded when Japan surrendered after the atomic bomb attacks on Nagasaki and Hiroshima. On November 1, 1945, Six Group, RCAF, stepped down from active service. The group had dropped 126,122 tons of bombs on the enemy and destroyed 116 enemy aircraft in action, while sinking or damaging 438 enemy ocean-going vessels of all sizes. It had lost 814 of its own planes and more than 3,500 of its men had been killed.

Air Chief Marshal Sir Arthur "Bomber" Harris, the Commander-in-Chief of Bomber Command, had this to say of McEwen and his all-Canadian group: "I regard this officer's contribution to the efficiency and effect of the bomber offensive as invaluable. In ability as in personality he stood out amongst his fellows. He is a great commander and the value of his work was a major contribution towards the success that was achieved. I cannot speak too highly of him or of his share, and his Group's share, in the common effort."

The group had earned its distinctive place among the formations of Bomber Command, a fact recognized by the Royal Air Force in an order which reserved the designation "No. Six Group" for Canada, should the need for another bomber command arise. In October, 1946, His Majesty, King George VI, gave his approval to the official badge of No. Six Group—a maple leaf superimposed on a York Rose. The motto emblazoned on the badge was Sollertia et Engenium—Initiative and Skill.

Winged Warfare

If Canada's Six Group had air crews who were considered the cream of the RCAF—and the country—it was entirely due to the efforts of men at home. McEwen had drilled his men in England and developed a superb force from good materials but other Canadians made sure that the RCAF got the right men. As the Second World War began breaking over Europe, the senior officers of the RCAF appraised the needs of far-ranging warfare and shifted the emphasis of their training programme to bombardment and air transport. In 1917 General Hugh Trenchard, chief of. the Royal Flying Corps, had given a lecture in which he had emphasized the correct use of air power in war. The role of the fighter plane, said the general, was a subsidiary one, important in defence, but wars were not won by defensive tactics. The bomber was the decisive weapon.

This was the message that Billy Bishop emphasized in his recruiting programme. He was the Canadian chiefly concerned with providing men for the new air force. By temperament, training, and outlook a fighter pilot, Bishop threw himself into the formidable task of recruiting bomber pilots with all the enthusiasm he had displayed in Flanders twenty years earlier. The Bishop name had lost none of its magic. His appeal for airmen aroused enthusiastic response: so enthusiastic that, while other services complained of man shortages, the Air Force for a time had to put applicants on a waiting list, since existing training facilities were swamped. Bishop worked a man-killing schedule. He made speeches, inspected graduating classes, awarded wings to successful air crew trainees, and worked long into the night planning for the expanding training facilities.

It was a little ironical that Bishop's new lesson should be contrary to the dreams that his own flying career inspired in the eager young recruits. Fired with the visions of individual exploits in the fast new fighter planes, the young men found the new concepts hard to accept. Many pilot-trainees were bitterly disappointed when, on graduation, they were assigned to further training as bomber pilots.

Bishop reiterated the importance of bombardment in his book Winged Warfare and its sequel Winged Peace. In a speech made to one graduating class he also said that he was sure that Canada's proud aerial traditions would be carried on. What he meant was that the bomber pilots of the forties were the true descendants of the fighter pilots of the twenties and would have equal opportunities for courage and service as his contemporaries had had. A glance at the record of just three of these "multi-engine" flyers who served this country in the Second World War proves that Bishop did not hope in vain.

Of all the unglamorous and tedious jobs tackled by the pilots of twin- and multi-engine aircraft, submarine patrol was probably the worst. In the vast stretches of ocean that were the hunting grounds of the U-boat, the job of finding the undersea craft was like looking for a needle in a haystack. Very early one summer morning, on June 7, 1944, before dawn had broken, K. O. Moore of the RCAF made history when he became the first pilot in the war to knock out two submarines in a single patrol. Moore was serving with the RAF's 244 Coastal Command Squadron. It was a calm night, and a full moon spread a silver sheen over the water as Moore lifted his big Liberator from its base at Ushant. Some hours later, still in the darkness, Moore's radar operator suddenly electrified the entire crew of the big plane with the report that he had made contact with a U-boat. The submarine was on the surface, probably charging its batteries in preparation for a day of stalking convoys. Moore swung the wheel to bring the

Nov. 15, 1943, photo shows an RCAF Consolidated model 32 Liberator GR Mk. V, serial no. 600, aircraft N, of No. 10 (Bomber Reconnaissance) Squadron, No. 1 Group, Eastern Air Command, taxiing on the inboard engines from an east coast dispersal. 600 began life as USAAF B-24D-70-CO, serial no. 42-40557, was supplied under Lend-Lease to the RAF as BZ755 then transferred to the RCAF. Note open bomb bay doors, anti-submarine radar antenna on the nose and standard Coastal Command finish. Dedicated to East Coast anti-submarine patrols, No. 10 (BR) Squadron, which won the nicknames "North Atlantic Squadron" and "Dumbo," finished the war having attacked 22 U-boats and sunk three. It was based at Gander, Nfld., at the time of this photo. Department of National Defence/PL-21811 plane on heading given by the radar man and at the same time called for full throttle.

In the bright moonlight the sub loomed ahead, her conning tower making a perfect silhouette against the moon-glow. The Liberator roared in to the kill. It was a set-piece attack. Moore's responses became almost automatic. How many times had he and his crew rehearsed this very thing in training! Scores of hours had been spent preparing this one moment, when each man would operate as an extension of the pilot's mind and will. "We passed dead over the conning tower and dropped six depth charges, a perfect straddle," Moore related later. The bombs, set for shallow depth, exploded almost on contact with the ocean. They blew the submarine right out of the water. Bedlam broke out inside the bomber as the gunners whooped and Moore's elated navigator and co-pilot pounded him on the back. Moore remembers that his comment was : "Now, let's get another one."

It was a bravado gesture, but the words were hardly of Moore's mouth when his bombardier shouted a warning. Dead ahead was the dark shape of another submarine. The plane had probably stumbled across the rendezvous of a wolf pack gathering off Ushant to prepare their attack on the crowded shipping around the British Isles.

This time the submarine fought back. Tracers from deck machine guns and 20-millimetre anti-aircraft cannon flashed past the speeding bomber as it bore in for a second time. The range was one mile and closing fast. The nose gunner of Moore's plane was already trading fire with the crews of the submarine's deck guns. Moore nursed the wheel and eased the plane lower. Then, "Bombs away!" shouted the bombardier. As Moore pulled the wheel back and the big plane zoomed over the sub, six more depth bombs splashed into the water on either side of the U-boat in another perfect straddle. The bombs detonated with a terrifying roar and the sea surged skyward in a gigantic explosion. The submarine's forward speed slackened and it began to list to starboard. When the plane circled back over the area, the bow of the U-boat rose from the water, pointed briefly at the stars, and slid from sight. On board the Liberator, the wireless operator was just completing his first strike report to base when he was told they had sunk another sub. "He thought we were kidding him," Moore related. Within twenty-two minutes Moore carried out two successful attacks against two different submarines. It was a freak combination of circumstances had placed the Liberator within striking range of the boats, whereas ninety-nine per cent of all the pilots on anti-submarine patrol cruised for months without even sighting one. There was nothing freakish about the precision and accuracy of the attack carried out by Moore and crew, though.

The young pilots who wore the blue uniform of the RCAF the Second World War possessed all the initiative, rage, and skill of the Canadians who blazed the trails of aerial warfare from 1914 to 1918. Canada's heavy bomber formation, Six Group, had many tales of heroism to tell. The two highest awards of the British Commonwealth—the Victoria Cross and the George Cross—were presented to members of Six Group during its wartime career. The recipient of the Victoria Cross was Andrew Charles Mynaraski, a twenty-eight-year-old wireless operator and air gunner. The base commander at Station Tholthorpe, Comlore A. D. Ross, was the George Cross winner. Mynarski was serving with 419 Squadron, a Lancaster unit. He had just been promoted and had replaced his sergeant's stripes with the narrow band of a pilot officer when, in June, 1944, bombers from his squadron were called on bomb a special target: the rail centre at Cambrai. The landings of D-Day had just taken place, and Six Group bombers had been assigned the task of disrupting rail communications to slow the arrival of German reinforcements in France.

Mynarski's plane was one of those that took off from Middleton St. George to bomb Cambrai. The bomber had begun its glide in to the target when the black shadow of a German JU-88 lunged at it out of the murky sky. A bright stream of fire hosed the Lancaster and cannon shell strikes lit the interior with lurid flashes of light. The enemy fighter made just one pass, then vanished into the darkness, like an indifferent barracuda fishtailing away from a dying whale.

"We're on fire, Skipper!" Mynarski heard the words over his earphones in his cramped radio operator's cabin. He glanced back quickly through the bomber. Beyond a wall of fire halfway to the stern he saw the tail gunner, Flying Officer George Brophy, preparing to leave his tiny, glass-enclosed tail turret. Just then both port engines of the crippled bomber failed.

The pilot, Flying Officer A. de Breyne, shouted over the intercom as he fought to maintain altitude to give his crew time to jump: "Bale out! Abandon ship! Hurry!" Their bombing run had been low, the plane was rapidly losing height and it was only a matter of seconds before it would be too late for the crew to use their parachutes. Mynarski clipped on his 'chute and headed for the nearest escape hatch. He watched several dark figures fall away from the bomber as he poised himself ready to leap. He glanced back for one last look into the burning bomber; his eyes met those of Brophy, still trapped inside the power turret. The loss of the port engines had caused a failure of the hydraulic gear and Brophy had been unable to turn his turret around to climb free. In his desperate struggle to escape he had broken off the manual release lever for such emergencies. The turret had now become his coffin.

Aug. 4, 1995, photo shows the Mynarski Memorial Lancaster in flight during an air show at CFB North Bay, Ont. This aircraft, built as Avro model 683 Lancaster B. Mk. X, serial no. FM213, by Victory Aircraft at Malton, Ont., in July 1945 as part of the last batch of Canadian-built Lancs, was stored until taken on RCAF strength June 21, 1946 and later converted to Lancaster 10 MR/MP (Maritime Reconnaissance/Maritime Patrol) standard and flown by 405 (Maritime Reconnaissance) Squadron and 107 Rescue Unit at Torbay, Nfld., before its retirement Nov. 6, 1963. The aircraft was saved from scrap by the Goderich Legion, which arranged for its display on a pedestal. It was later sold to the Canadian Warplane Heritage Museum, at Ancaster, Ont., and restored to flying condition in the markings of Lancaster B Mk. X serial no. KB726, coded KR*A, of 419 "Moose" (Bomber) Squadron, in which P/O Andrew Mynarski won his posthumous Victoria Cross during a raid on Cambrai, France, on the night of June 12, 1944.
Department of National Defence/DND95-219-46

Without hesitation, Mynarski plunged through the flames that separated him from the trapped gunner. His clothing and parachute took fire, and with burned and blistered hands he tugged at the metal framework of the gun turret, trying to move it by brute force. Hydraulic fluid drenched his clothing, which burst into flames. Still he fought to save his companion. "It's no use!" Brophy shouted above the roar of the flames. "Get going. You can't help me anyway, I've had it." His hands seared to the bone, Mynarski finally admitted defeat. He staggered back through the flames to the escape hatch. Turning towards the trapped gunner, he stood at attention and saluted. When he jumped it was too late. Mynarski was a human torch when he left the plane. Somehow, he managed to pull the D string of his parachute, but the fire had burned away most of the canopy, and, with clothing and parachute still burning, he fell at a tremendous speed. On the ground, French peasants working in the fields watched him fall and later described the parachute as a fireball. He hit the ground and lay still.

By a miracle Brophy survived the terrifying ordeal. After Mynarski jumped, the pilotless bomber flew on on its remaining engines, trailing smoke and flame and gradually losing altitude. When it finally crashed, Brophy was hurled clear of his tiny prison, surviving what had appeared to be certain death. Mynarski's heroism was not discovered until after the war, when Brophy and the other members of the crew who were released from prison camps told the story. As a result Six Group won its first Victoria Cross, awarded posthumously to Pilot Officer Andrew Mynarski of Winnipeg.

Less then twenty days after Mynarski's magnificent attempt to save his companion, another crippled RCAF bomber, Halifax "C" for Charlie, from 425 (Alouette) Squadron, was struggling home from a successful attack against the German flying bomb launching sites in the Foret d'Eawy. One engine had been shot out, but it seemed that the pilot, Sergeant M. J. P. Lavoie, would be able to bring the Halifax down to a safe landing. It was early in the morning of June 28 when the wail of the crash siren brought everyone to the flight line at Station Tholthorpe to watch the pilot nurse his crippled bird down to earth. Among the spectators was the station commander, Air Commodore A. D. Ross, a veteran pilot with lengthy service in the RCAF.

Lavoie's landing was good and everyone began to breathe more easily when suddenly a tire blew out and the huge plane, still rolling at a good clip, veered sharply and ploughed into a parked aircraft which had just been loaded with ten 500-pound bombs. There was a deafening explosion and a ball of flame billowed from the wreckage. Crash wagons roared across the field towards the wreck. Commodore Ross, who was closest to the crash, could see that the pilot was either trapped or dazed by the concussion. He dashed into the flames and, with the help of two other Flight Sergeant J. R. M. St. Germain, the bomb-aimer from another Halifax which had just landed, and Corporal M. Marquet, a ground crewman, pulled the injured airman from the wreckage. The fire had reached the bomb and the blasts of the exploding bombs hurled the rescuers and rescued to the ground. Just as the roar of the explosions subsided, Ross heard a faint cry from the tail turret of "C" for Charlie. Immediately he dashed back to the burning plane. Helped by St. Germain and Aircraft M. M. McKenzie and R. R. Wolfe from the station crash tender, the officer used an axe to smash the plexiglass the turret to free the gunner, Sergeant C. G. Rochon. Just then another bomb exploded and a flying piece of metal sheared off Ross's right hand. Quickly fashioning a torniquet around his wrist, he walked calmly across the field to the medical centre to have his wound tended.

127

Thanks to Ross's alertness and courage, the entire of the crashed bomber was saved. His leadership in directing the rescue was also credited with saving other aircraft parked nearby. Air Commodore Ross was awarded the George Cross, given for acts of bravery which do not place in battle. Flight Sergeant St. Germain and Corporall Marquet were awarded the George Medal for their part in the rescue, and Aircraftsmen McKenzie and Wolfe received the British Empire Medal.

The King of the Pathfinders

The Fauquier family was well-to-do, and John attended

fashionable Ashbury College, where he became head boy and was noted as
something of a mathematical wizard. He had shown a strong interest in medicine
at school, but on graduation he left the family mansion for Montreal, where he
became a successful bond salesman. John Fauquier was no less successful in his
social life and became something of a lion among Montreal's young set. He
found an outlet for his restlessness in speed: he owned both an automobile and
a motorcycle. Then he joined Montreal's Light Aeroplane Club. This casual
decision changed his entire life, for Fauquier was one of those rare men who are
indeed "born to fly." Flying so appealed to him that, early in the 1920's, he
turned his back forever on St. James Street, the bond business, and Montreal's
social life. He set up a small bush airline, Commercial Airways, operating out of
Noranda, the centre of mining operations and prospecting for northern Quebec.
The decision was all the more momentous since Fauquier was married now. It
was no easy thing for a man to turn his back on seven years in a lucrative business
and strike out in a field that was still in the experimental stage. But while the
bond business returned a handsome salary, it had little to offer a man of
Fauquier's temperament.

Fauquier started his airline with two airplanes, a Waco and a Fairchild. In
the late 1920's commercial flying was still in the early stages of evolution, but
Fauquier thrived under the constant challenge offered by both the elements and
the business competition. It was a rugged life. The flying community of Noranda
consisted of four small companies, all located on the same lake, and all operated
by young people. They were a zesty lot, full of enthusiasm and dreams of the
expansion of the north, far different from some of the bored young sophisticates
whom Fauquier had known in Montreal.

As both owner and chief pilot of the airline, Fauquier had all the work that
his active nature desired. The heavy work of wrestling cargoes into the planes
toughened his muscles, and the primitive conditions taught him independence
and the knack of practical invention born of necessity. His wife often accompanied
him on the long flights over the silent forests and lakes of northern Quebec and

Ontario. By the time the war began Fauquier had logged more 300,000 miles in the air.

On November 1, 1939, he enlisted in the RCAF as a flight lieutenant and took an instructor's course at Camp Borden and Trenton. For a time it looked as though Johnny Farquier's war would be spent in training school, teaching rookies the first principles of flying. In those early days of the war, Canada required many experienced pilots to instruct the thousands of youngsters who had enlisted in the Air Force under the Commonwealth Air Training Plan.

Then in June, 1941, the man who was destined to be known as the "King of the Pathfinders," was transferred England to a glider and paratroop training school. September of that year saw him posted to No. 405 Squadron, a bomber formation. Fauquier's first operations were performed in a Halifax bomber, a machine that was very difficult to handle. In later years he remembered the first he ever saw the big, four-motor Lancaster bomber would carry him to fame: he was guiding his formation home from a particularly tough raid when "the Lancasters came streaming by, and were home forty-five minutes ahead of me. I said to myself, 'I've got to get my hands on one of those.' "

He did not have long to wait, for No. 405 Squadron notified that it was to be re-equipped with Lancasters. "You can imagine our relief when we knew we were getting this superior aircraft, which in the end carried the heaviest bomb in the European theatre, the Grand Slam. Morale went up fantastically as the Lancaster proved herself to us. This was a big aircraft, and she flew as easily and as dexterously as a Tiger Moth. The Lanc had no bad habits . . . you could dive the Lancaster at phenomenal speeds to escape the cone of enemy searchlights."

By February, 1942, he had performed so well as a bomber pilot and flight-leader that he was promoted to the rank of wing commander and given command of the squadron. A Distinguished Flying Cross accompanied the promotion. The citation had this to say of Fauquier: "Throughout the many sorties in which he has participated this officer has displayed the highest quality of courage and leadership. His ability and grim determination to inflict the maximum damage on the enemy have won the admiration of the squadron he commands. Wing Commander Fauquier took part in the two raids on Essen when a thousand of our aircraft operated each time. He is an exceptional leader." Fauquier's "grim determination to inflict the maximum damage on the enemy" soon established for 405 Squadron the record of dropping the largest bomb tonnage ever to fall on enemy targets from the bomb bays of a single squadron.

John Fauquier was gifted with the same dash and ability that had distinguished Canada's fighter pilots in the First War. He was a good pilot, hence a "lucky" pilot; he was also a popular pilot among the airmen who flew with him. One of their stories told how Johnny Fauquier once used his heavy bomber as a fighter plane, in order to protect his high-flying squadron mates.

It was over Bremen, in June, 1942. Heavy concentrations of flak and night fighters were creating havoc in the formation, which was being coned by batteries of searchlights. To avoid the heavy fire, 405's pilots had to take violent evasive action. This spoiled the chance of each plane's bomb-aimer to line up his sights on the targets far below, and to miss the targets would mean that the squadron would have to return another night and again face the maelstrom of cannon shells and flak. As their leader, Fauquier was directing the onslaught of the bomber formation, and he realized that something must be done to give his aircrew respite from the barrage. Picking out an assembly of flak batteries and searchlights near the bomber's objective, he shot his huge craft down from 12,000 feet, at the same urging his gunners to blast the ground defences with heavy machine guns. Handling the huge bomber as though it a fighter, Fauquier ranged over the ground defences, heedless of the hail of machine gun and light cannon fire brought to bear on his plane. He diverted the fire of the ground defences to himself and at the same time smashed the lights that were pinning his other aircraft to the sky like moths. It was a fantastic feat for a heavy bomber. Fauquier's ground-strafing sortie was the talk of Six Group and Bomber Command for a long time. Later, when asked if he experienced fear on such missions, he said: "A man who wasn't frightened lacked imagination, and without imagination he couldn't be a first class warrior. Let's face it: good men were frightened. Especially between briefing and take-off. bravest man I knew used to go to bed right after briefing, and refuse to eat. Sick with fear. Any man that frightened who goes to the target is brave."

In the summer of 1942 Fauquier's squadron, now part of No. 8 Pathfinder Group, took part in the massive assault on the German city port of Hamburg. The Pathfinders were a new concept in heavy bombardment. Their job to fly ahead of the bombers and mark the route and target with flares and "Christmas trees" of tinsel-like phosphorous that hung in the sky like traffic lights. It was dangerous work, probing alone into enemy-held sky. Under Fauquier's leadership the squadron had become one of most successful in the Pathfinder Group. For the raid on Hamburg, besides his duty as Pathfinder, Fauquier way appointed to act as deputy Master Bomber. His task was to fly over the target throughout the raid, directing the incoming streams of bombers to untouched bombing areas, much as a traffic policeman directs automobiles. The Master Bomber had to remain constantly over the target area, braving flak and the night fighters throughout the entire while the aircraft actually engaged in bombing could look forward to making their bomb run and immediately getting clear of the battle area.

It was all part of the new tactics devised by the RAF and RCAF for night bombing. Instead of using the stretched-out formations which covered a broad expanse of sky on the to the target and back, planes flew in to the target area number of small waves from all points of the compass. They rarely saw each other until, like raindrops, they had massed together over the objective to saturate the ground below with bombs. The new technique lessened the dangerous time over target for individual aircraft and also made it more difficult for the enemy interceptors to find the attackers in the darkness, since there was no actual formation to assault. But the German Fighter Control had soon learned the role played by the Master Bomber in the successful attacks and German fighters began cruising the aerial arenas, searching for the lone plane from which the Master Bomber plotted his next moves. Fauquier therefore had the most dangerous assignment of all during the Hamburg operation.

He once described another aspect of the raid on Hamburg:

> We were after military objectives, the seaport, armament
> works and so on, but there was another kind of policy at
> work: demoralize the people, don't let them sleep, make them
> homeless, break their will. It's not the kind of thing we ever
> bragged about. But those people were at war with us, and they
> were very serious about it. Hitler, you know, called us "Air
> Pirates." Some of us were to be beheaded if we were captured.
>
> From a CBC documentary film, *The Last of the Lancasters.*

Perhaps the greatest tribute to Fauquier's ability was his assignment to one of the most critical and top secret raids of the war. Since 1935, German scientists, under the direction of rocket expert Wernher von Braun, had been experimenting with rocket-propelled guided missiles at a remote spot on the Baltic Sea called Peenemunde. The entire project had been kept top secret, even from members of the General Staff, for a number of years. As the war neared the end of its third year, Hitler began more and more to rely on Peenemunde to come up with the miracle weapon that he needed if he were to win. But Allied air intelligence had discovered Hitler's secret. The sharp eyes of Flight Officer Constance Babington-Smith, the girl who had the job of evaluating the pictures taken by reconnaissance aircraft, spotted a tiny black smudge on the runways at Peenemunde. The smudge did not resemble the normal runway wear and tear from conventional aircraft, so more high-flying Spitfires were sent out to take more pictures. These photos showed oddly shaped aircraft parked around the runways, and the rocket secret of the Nazis was out. The black smudge was the carbon left by the blast of burning gases ejected from the tail pipes of the experimental jets. The Allies had uncovered the launching site of the Germans' robot flying bomb, the V-1 (called "The Doodlebug" by British fighter pilots) which for a time rained death and destruction on England. The inaccurate but destructive Doodlebug was only the forerunner, however, of a far deadlier weapon, the V-2, a heavy guided missile.

The Allied Command decreed that Peenemunde must be destroyed. Canada's Six Group was called on to provide a large share of the bombing force of six hundred aircraft assigned to the mission. Details of the raid were kept so secret that even the air crews taking part did not know what they were attacking. They were told that Peenemunde was turning out improved radar sets for night fighters. Bomber Command chose its top Master Bombers to conduct the raid: the RAF's fabled Group Captain Searby and the RCAF's Johnny Fauquier. Their orders were simple: they must splash this target on the first try. If they failed they would have to go back again and again if necessary, but Peenemunde must be destroyed. It was to be a maximum effort attack.

No one got much sleep at Castle Dismal as Black Mike McEwen and Six Group's staff planned the attack with Fauquier. It was decided that the attacking force would use the same route followed by formations heading for Berlin, and would be accompanied by a host of planes which would continue to the German capital after the actual attackers had made a last-minute turn north towards the North Sea and Peenemunde. The attack was launched on the night of August 17, 1943. The deception worked, for during the early part of the raid German night fighters had been ordered to points inland to intercept what was considered to be a large-scale attack on Berlin. Fauquier was over Peenemunde throughout the entire attack. He made seventeen dangerous passes over the target, directing the incoming waves of bombers and assessing the damage on the ground. It was a clear, moonlight night, ideal for flak and fighters. Seasoned bomber pilots still talk about the job Fauquier did. For thirty-five minutes he remained over the target, dodging flak and fighters, sweeping in at varying altitudes, until the last bomber was on its way back to Britain, and the workshops, laboratories, and living quarters at Peenemunde were a mass of blazing wreckage.

When the last heavy had unloaded its cargo of bombs, Canada's Master Bomber turned for home. German fighters, fooled by the diversionary tactics earlier, were now either on the scene, or lying in wait for the bombers along the homeward route. Furious at being tricked, they hurled themselves at the bombers, their machine guns and cannon lacing the night sky with bright pink tracers. Plane after plane faltered and plunged to alien territory far below. Before the night was over forty-one of the bombers had been shot down, ten of them manned by Canadian crews. But the attack had been a complete success. Peenemunde and its rockets lay in ruins. The worst consequence for the Germans was that many of their leading experts in jet propulsion and rocketry were killed in the raid. The attack delayed the development of the V-1 and V-2 rocket bombs by a year, thus saving London from complete devastation. When rockets were finally launched against that city they neither the range nor the explosive qualities of the weapons that

Oct. 21, 1943, photo shows an Avro model 683 Lancaster heavy bomber towering over an approaching airman on the flight line. Location unknown.

were destroyed at Peenemunde. For his night's work Johnny Fauquier was awarded the Distinguished Service Order.

By January, 1944, Fauquier had completed his second tour of operations with 405 Squadron and handed over command to Wing Commander R. J. Lane, DSO, DFC. Farquier had flown at least thirty-eight sorties with the squadron. During his term as commander he had built the unit into one of the best, in a group that had many crack squadrons. In March a bar was added to his DSO, in recognition of his work with Number 405.

Fauquier's formula for leadership was simple: he never asked another pilot to do something he would not do himself. Time after time he chose the most dangerous task of a mission. He was the "follow me" type of leader rather than the "get going" kind. No armchair commander, he won respect and loyalty of his men by his own courage.

While the average man would have been content to put his feet under a desk for the rest of the war after completing two tours of operations, Fauquier was cut from the same cloth as Billy Bishop, Barker, and Collishaw. Promoted to the rank of air commodore in June, 1944, he voluntarily reverted in rank to group captain so that he could begin his third tour of operations, this time as the commanding officer of an RAF unit.

Number 617 "Dambuster" Squadron, RAF, was a unit composed of specialists in precision bombing. The Dambusters had originally been formed for the special task destroying the Mohne, Eder, and Sorpe dams in order to flood the Low Countries and disrupt German communications. Now they ranged over the Continent, hitting special targets with the brand new 22,000-pound Grand Slam bombs, the biggest ever used in Europe. These powerful weapons were still in short supply. Fauquier, rather than see them wasted in misses, developed the practice of acting as Master Bomber for the squadron, flying low over the target and braving the flak to direct while the others circled and watched. This, a radical departure from the usual methods of the Dambusters, was precision bombing at its most refined. Fauquier would call on only as many planes as he needed to destroy the target; the rest would be sent home with their precious Grand Slams intact and ready for another day. This way the squadron destroyed pin-point targets such as viaducts, rail bridges, roundhouses, submarine pens, and the last of the German battleships. Fauquier described one of the Dambusters' assignments, the destruction of the Neinberge Bridge:

We loaded eighteen Lancs with these bombs [Grand Slams] to get the Neinberge bridge, over which supplies travelled to the enemy front lines. I was in a Mosquito down low beside the bridge, and was struck by a fit of economy. Why throw away eighteen of these expensive, handmade bombs on one bridge? I called in three of my fellows, while the rest circled. The result was a sensation. Two bombs hit, one at each end. The bridge actually rose in the air, intact, and I could see right under it. Then the third bomb hit the structure square, as it flew through the air. We could try that again a thousand times, and never do it.

The Dambusters' last raid was on Adolf Hitler's personal headquarters at Berchtesgaden:

Perhaps the most satisfying raid by the Lancasters of the Dambusters was the last. The attack on Hitler's country cottage, of no military value, was a salutary moment in the history of this aircraft. How many nations had been threatened from Berchtesgaden? How many decisions made on this spot, to annihilate millions of souls?

Hitler's "cottage," built of heavy stone and concrete, and equipped with deep reinforced cottage bomb shelters, was pulverized by the Lancaster attack.

Fauquier's skill left even the veteran Dambusters a little in awe of their Canadian commander. As one pilot put it: "He plants those bombs like he was threading a needle." They all agreed that the additional bar to his DSO— equivalent of three of the coveted Orders—was more than merited. Besides these awards, Fauquier won a DFC, the Croix de guerre with Palm, and was created a Chevalier of the Légion d'honneur, to become one of the most decorated Canadian aviators to emerge from the Second World War. But it was the British press that gave him an unofficial award by which he became world famous. An enterprising Fleet Street reporter called Fauquier the "King of the Pathfinders," in a story he wrote about the Canadian. No one ever contested the title.

The Loner

They called him "Screwball," sometimes in friendship but more often in anger, tinged with envy. He was the greatest fighter pilot Canada produced in the Second World War, a lonely who angered superiors and antagonized wing-mates with his proud awareness of his own worth as a flyer and his often biting comments on the ability of fellow aviators. George "Buzz" Beurling, of Verdun, Quebec, was, in many ways, a man out of touch with the times, an ardent indi-vidualist in the era of the organization man, a "loner" who preferred it that way. "He was a very difficult man to understand ... he got your back up," said a one-time Spitfire pilot who flew with Beurling at Malta. "A remote, brooding lad who showed great individual promise but whose temperament was not suited to our style of team fighting," said ace combat pilot and Beurling's commander, Group Captain "Johnnie" Johnson. "He was a man without ambition for promotion, who just wanted to do the things he did best, fly and fight," was the comment of Air ViceMarshal Clifford M. "Black Mike" McEwen.

"I have no other interests but flying ... I will always fly," Beurling once said of himself. In temperament Buzz Beurling resembled another famous Canadian aviator once described as introspective, Bill Barker. There was even a marked physical resemblance, and both men were noted for a frankness about their own ability that often offended listeners. They meant no offence. They were merely stating a fact well known to them, and obvious to anyone who cared to look at the record. However, while Barker's rebellion against a posting to a soft job behind the front lines was understood and indulged, such was not the case with Beurling. When Beurling fought his war, fighter tactics had changed drastically from the days of Bishop and Barker. The era of single combat had been ended by the huge dogfights over France in 1918, when fleets of aircraft fought pitched battles for control of the skies. By the time the Second World War began, the smallest unit of combat was an "element" of two aircraft, one to make the kill, the other to protect the tail of the first. With the heavier armament of fighters, and the greatly increased speeds, it was all but impossible for a lone pilot to carry out a successful attack and guard his own tail at the same time; an enemy fighter could appear as if by magic.

It is all the more remarkable, therefore, that Beurling clung to the old loner system and that, for him, it worked. Only a unique combination of fantastic marksmanship, superb flying skill, and pure luck made his survival possible. Beurling scored most of his thirty-one victories as a loner. He resented a wing man as an encumbrance, a feeling soon transmitted to any luckless pilot assigned to him. This attitude, and his general demeanour, widened the breach between Beurling and his fellow airmen. There are some people who lack the art of human communication, the ability to establish a warm relationship with their fellow men. This lack does not mean that such persons do not yearn for friendship, but pride, and an inability to allow themselves to be caught off guard, prevent them from taking the first step. Consequently they shrink within themselves, adopting a stern and sometimes cynical attitude towards their fellows.

Buzz Beurling was such a man. He was different from most of the other pilots who manned the Spitfires and Hurricanes; different because of his skill and because, as he said, "To most of these fellows, the Air Force is just an interlude." The majority of Beurling's fellow pilots.were fulfilling their duty to their country in time of war. But flying, to Beurling, was a way of life, an end in itself. As a boy he had fixed his eyes on the sky, and, when other teen-age boys were having their first dates and learning the latest dance steps, Beurling had his nose buried in a pre-flight manual.

So some of them called him "Screwball," and the nickname stung despite his apparently casual acceptance of it. "I had a reputation for being a wild flyer," he once said. "And I always rubbed people the wrong way." This was one explanation for the nickname. There were others. His reefusal to accept a promotion to a commissioned rank, for example, was inconceivable to most men who strove for advancement. There was also his feud with the RCAF and its way of describing a plane as a "screwball kite."

Even as a boy in Verdun, Beurling's hunting forays contributed to his later deadly skill as a fighter pilot. "I was always thinking of angles of fire," he once explained. The flight of a covey of birds before the muzzle of his shotgun taught him to lead a target and make lightning calculations on speed and trajectory.

It has been said of genius that its main component is single-mindedness. While genius has always been associated with creative ability, there are those who claim that technicians (such as performing musicians) can also achieve that exalted status. If such a lofty phrase can be applied to the romantic, but purely technical, skill of flying, then Beurling, like the young Mozart, was a genius.

Beurling first flew at the age of nine, when a pilot at the airport near his home took him up "for a flip" in exchange for chores performed around the hangars. Later, he started building model aircraft and selling them to his friends. As soon as he earned $10, he spent it on flying lessons. He first took over the controls of an airplane at fourteen and had soloed at sixteen. While his parents did not discourage him, his father refused to give him money to be "wasted" on his single passion. He received his pilot's licence just before the war and, in 1939, passed an examination for a commercial licence. The licence itself was refused because he was considered too young for commercial flying.

Beurling's determination was such that, when he decided to learn all there was to know about aerobatics, he went to the best man available for tuition, Germany's First World War ace, Ernst Udet. "To me, he was the greatest flyer of all time," Beurling related years later. And there is little doubt that Udet had a pronounced influence on the young pilot. The tall, blond boy saved his money and rode a freight train to the West Coast in order to take instruction from the famous sky fighter.

Even as a youth, Beurling's confidence in his own ability heralded a difficult relationship between himself and Canada's air force. There was a competition in aerobatics at an air show in Edmonton, and the eighteen-year-old Beurling had entered against a field of veteran flyers, including two pilots of the RCAF. Beurling won and, when he stepped up to collect his prize, angered senior RCAF officers by stating brashly: "If that's the best the RCAF can do, it'd better get some new pilots." The statement repelled everyone in hearing, and yet it was more the attempt of a youngster trying to impress his seniors than an intended insult. It was youthful bragging, the retort of a boy who had been so preoccupied with his own ambitions that he had never learned how to wait politely for recognition.

When the war started the RCAF turned Beurling down when he tried to enlist. In later years, he bitterly asserted that the reason was his comment at the Edmonton air show, but the causes were deeper than that. He had a brilliant but unstable record as a private pilot, and his years and educational background were against him. In that first wave of recruiting that followed the outbreak of the Second World War, RCAF standards were very high, since the force could afford to be selective. In the aerial team the RCAF was trying to build there would be no room for loners who appeared to scorn authority. Later, the educational standards were pared down to a level that conformed with Beurling's grades, but by that time he had gone his own way.

Following the RCAF's refusal, Beurling tried to enlist as a pilot with the Chinese Air Force in that country's war with Japan. He slipped into the United States, planning to take ship from San Francisco for the Orient. However, the

United States Immigration authorities picked him up for illegal entry and sent him back to Canada. Then he tried to join the Air Force of Finland, through the Finnish consul in Montreal (Finland was fighting Russia), but his parents refused to give him the necessary permission.

Again he tried the RCAF and was refused because of his lack of formal schooling. Then Beurling hit on the plan of joining the RAF. He heard of a Chilean cargo vessel, the *Valparaiso*, which needed sailors. The ship was one of a convoy taking munitions to Glasgow, and, half an hour after he asked the captain for a job, the ship sailed with Beurling aboard. Off the coast of Ireland the convoy ran into a wolf pack of submarines, and seven ships were sunk. But the luck that was to follow the young Canadian through the war was with him, and the creaky old *Valparaiso* arrived unharmed.

The ship had barely docked when Beurling was ashore, presenting himself to the nearest RAF recruiting officer. "I'm sorry, son, but you haven't even got your birth certificate with you. I can't do anything for you without papers," the officer told him. (Beurling only had his pilot's log book, showing 250 hours.)

"I'll go back and get them," replied the Canadian. The "errand" took him back across the submarine-infested Atlantic, and again, the U-boats were waiting. Another ship was torpedoed and sunk, but Beurling's luck was holding. After five days at home, he again boarded the *Valparaiso* for the return voyage. This time the submarines failed to find the convoy and all the ships made it to Glasgow.

"It's my Canadian!" the surprised RAF recruiting officer cried when Beurling strode into his office. Beurling was signed up immediately.

At first life in the service was a disappointment. Beurling was assigned to a labour squad that spent its time filling in the bomb craters on RAF fields. Then came ground school, a nightmare for Beurling with his lack of education. He spent long, off-duty hours boning up on mathematics and navigation to catch up with his better-educated fellows and pass the course. The fear of failure and his own determination carried him through and, while not a brilliant student, mustered a passing grade.

In the flight training that followed, Beurling made up for the sneers he had endured in ground school by his rapid assimilation of skills in night flying, combat tactics, and aerial gunnery. With a spotless flying record, he graduated as sergeant pilot and was assigned to No. 403 Squadron, a Hurricane unit, on December 16, 1941.

He did not remain with the squadron long. Number 403 was designated an RCAF unit, and Beurling, as a member the RAF, was transferred to another RAF squadron, No. 242. Number 242 Squadron was a Canadian unit serving with the RAF Fighter Command. It may be that his superiors thought it would be best for Beurling to be given a berth among his countrymen, but it turned out differently. Beurling, never one to curb his tongue, spoke out bitterly again the RCAF and antagonized a number of his squadron mates. His brashness was not appreciated by many of the pilots 242 Squadron, a veteran unit which had seen hard fighting during the Battle of Britain, and in France. Real trouble began when he to locked horns with his flight leader, a Permanent Force squadron leader who had little sympathy for bold young prodigies. As a result, Beurling was given the "tail-end Charlie" position in the flight. This was a particularly dangerous spot, yet it always went to newcomers, probably on the rather cold-blooded theory that they were the most expendable. Charlie had the job of weaving back and forth across the stern of the formation, keeping a weather-eye out for enemy fighters. Since most attacks usually developed from astern, Charlie was usually the first man to be hit if the flight was bounced by enemy planes.

On one of his first missions, Beurling deepened the gap between himself and his flight leader. Years later he described the incident: "We were in the air, with our tails in the sun, and vulnerable to attack, when I called up and reported Huns." Whether it was pure hunch (Beurling later developed a sixth sense about the presence of danger that saved his life on more than one occasion) or whether he had actually caught a fleeting glimpse of a German formation is not known. A search of the sky revealed no threat and Beurling was roasted by his squadron leader for breaking radio silence and "causing trouble by reporting Huns that weren't there.

"Five minutes later we got bounced and I got shot," Beurling recalled; a splinter of cannon shell grazed Beurling's ribs during the fight. Nevertheless, he downed his first enemy aircraft in that battle.

The average man would have left well alone, either waiting for an apology from his commander, or at least savouring the knowledge that he had been right. Not Beurling. The moment the flight landed at its base he stormed out of his cockpit and buttonholed the erring squadron leader right on the flight line. Before the rest of the pilots, he blistered the older man's ears and came dangerously close to insubordination.

Things became more strained between Beurling and his senior officers after this incident, and when an opportunity arrived to transfer out of the squadron he accepted with alacrity. A young, recently married pilot had been assigned to an overseas posting, and Beurling volunteered to replace him in May, 1942.

"You must be able to take off from an aircraft carrier—can you do that?" he was asked.

"Yes, sir."

The next day, Beurling arrived at the point of embarkation to board a cargo boat with thirty-five other pilots. In the hold were thirty-six brand new Spitfire V's, armed with four 20-millimeter cannon. The ship carried the flyers and their planes to Gibraltar. There, the planes were assembled and the pilots learned their destination—Malta. Malta was a key base for British shipping passing through the Mediterranean. The island fortress had proved to be a thorn in the side of Fascist ambitions, for the territory could be also used as a staging area for sea and air attacks against Axis supply lines to North Africa. Because of this, Hitler ordered that the island be "neutralized" by air attack. Day and night, German bomber squadrons smashed the docks, airfields, and homes on the island, and German and Italian fighters worked to destroy the last remnants of the island's fighter defence. But a daring plan to reinforce the island's air defences had been devised. The carrier HMS *Eagle*, heavily escorted by cruisers and destroyers, would fight its way across the Mediterranean and launch the Spitfires at sea. The planes would fly the remainder of the way to Malta.

At the launching point, the pilots were briefed: "You will Maintain absolute radio silence, except in case of distress, when you can transmit 'Mayday.' Good luck."

The planes were launched in groups of eight. Beurling was in the third group. The take-off from the narrow, pitching deck of the *Eagle* was a new experience for RAF pilots trained on the long, grassy airstrips of England. Also Spitfires were not then designed for carrier operations and required a much longer take-off run to become airborne. But on this occasion the forward speed of the carrier and a brisk, thirty-knot wind compensated for the short take-off. With brakes locked on, Beurling gunned his engine to full throttle until the tail of his fast little fighter lifted off the deck. Then, brakes off: the plane lunged forward, dipped towards the sea, and soared into the sky.

Minutes dragged into hours as the planes droned over the blue ocean, skirting the Axis-held Algerian coast and boring steadily towards Malta. Then, fifteen minutes from their destination, garbled snatches of conversation began to crackle in the earphones of the pilots—mixed German and English voices. On Malta, ground control radar had picked up the incoming Spitfires and, simultaneously, a large number of blips rising over Sicily: German and Italian planes, forming for another air strike at Malta. It was now a race to see who would arrive first, the Spitfires, with their greenhorn pilots and almost empty gas tanks, or the enemy. "Hullo, Condor Leader, steer 081 and get a move on." The urgency in the voice of the ground control officer could not be denied. There it was below, the vast pile of rock that was Malta, with its battered Takali airfield.

Six Spitfires of the island's meagre defence forces scrambled to provide top cover for the incoming aircraft, as one by one the newcomers landed, to be immediately surrounded by a wild-looking, half-naked mob of shouting ground crewmen, stripped to the waist in the oppressive heat. A rigger leaped on Beurling's wing to guide him into a bomb-proof revetment. There the plane was swung around and the Canadian was literally lifted out of the cockpit. His belongings, packed in the wings and fuselage of the plane, were dumped unceremoniously in the dust while belts of cannon shells were loaded in the wing pods. A chain of mechanics was formed, passing cans of gasoline to a crewman who splashed the precious fluid into the Spitfire's tanks. Another pilot brushed past Beurling and climbed into the plane. Impatiently he waved away the ground crewmen and gunned the plane down the dusty field, the propeller blast throwing dust and sand into Beurling's face. The ground crewmen vanished as rapidly as they had appeared and the confused Canadian only realized what was happening when bombs began to burst on the field and a section of Messerschmitt 109's swung low over the field, their guns kicking up fountains of dirt. With the other equally bewildered Eagle pilots, Beurling sprinted to a bomb shelter.

"Welcome to Malta," grinned a haggard corporal.

Beurling had wanted action, and now he was finding plenty of it. Across the field, a Junkers 88 that had been caught in the guns of a Spitfire emitted a cloud of oily smoke and crashed into a building. Flames spread to RAF bombers parked nearby. Wave after wave of German and Italian planes roared over the field and the sky rained chunks of metal. Parachutes floated serenely through the columns of smoke and the twisting, diving airplanes. The newcomers were all but deafened by the incessant roar of bursting bombs, the clatter of machine guns, and the whine of motors.

Suddenly it was over. Beurling walked out to the flight line to wait for his plane. A weary pilot, climbing from a battered Spit, saw the Canadian: "If you're waiting for your plane, forget it. The pilot who was flying it got the chop."

Beurling arrived early in the summer of 1942 when the air attack was at its height. He endured the sleepless nights, the bad food, and the constant strain, and thrived. In the siege conditions of the island, pilots lost weight rapidly because of the shortage of food. The average menu consisted of a slab of fried corned beef, a few dates, and olives. Pilots were issued a special ration of two spoonsful of shredded carrot soaked in cod liver oil, for vitamins. The pilots—both officers and men—lived in caves carved out of an old chalk quarry near the airfield. This abnormal life trimmed Beurling's husky body down from 177 to 126 pounds, but this was the fulfilment of all his dreams and ambitions. He said later that he would give "ten years of my life to relive those six months in Malta.... Every time you went up the sky was full of Germans."

Beurling's loss of weight was also a result of the alerts, when pilots, in flying gear, sat for an hour at a time in the cockpits of their planes, waiting for the word to scramble. The heat was so intense that ground crewmen rigged rough tents and soaked the canvas in water to escape the heat while they waited for the planes to be launched. But there was no respite from the broiling sun for the pilots as they sat in their open cockpits, soaked in perspiration and dizzy from the heat.

Yet, here on Malta, Beurling made the most significant friendships of his life. These sergeant pilots, unshaven, gaunt with fatigue, and thinned from the restricted diet, were his kind of people. Never in sympathy with military courtesy, Beurling liked the informality of Malta's front line squadrons. His own squadron, No. 249, included a number of Canadians. Beurling's closest companion was another Canadian, Jean Paradis, with whom, on quiet days, he would swim in the clear blue waters of the Mediterranean, and talk. When Paradis was killed it was a cruel blow to the lonely Beurling.

"Scramble! Bandits, 20,000 feet. Twenty plus big boys [bombers] and forty plus fighters." The twelve Spitfires on the alert line raced across the dusty airstrip and climbed rapidly on a westerly heading. After the hammering attack that greeted him on arrival, Beurling found ten days of peace on Malta as the enemy withheld their forces. But now the war was on again, and Beurling got his first taste of action on the big rock.

The Spits climbed steadily, racing for the advantage of height before closing with the enemy. The sky was sparkling blue with only wisps of cloud providing little cover for the outnumbered RAF fighters. They split into two formations of six planes each, while the pilots searched the sky for the oncoming formation of sixty raiders. Then: "Tally-ho, bandits at four o'clock."

A collection of bulky shapes: Junkers 88's. But where were the fighters? Half the British formation peeled off to attack the big boys while the remaining six Spitfires, with Beurling, remained aloft, waiting to intercept the inevitable fighters. At last a cluster of dots, ME-109's, could be seen barrelling down towards the fight below. The six Spitfires lunged forward and the two formations blended in a wild mêlée of circling, diving planes.

The yellowish-green camouflage of a Messerschmitt showed momentarily in Beurling's gun sight and he thumbed the firing button eagerly. Missed. With stick and rudder bar he rolled the Spit on its back, chasing the elusive German. "Now." The 109 was broadside. The cannon thundered again, but the wily German half-rolled and slipped away. Impatiently Beurling corrected his first angle, intent on his prey. Suddenly fire flashed across his field of vision and a cluster of holes appeared in his wing. He had failed to notice an Italian Macchi 202 stalking him from behind.

The over-eager Italian overshot as Beurling throttled back. Then the situation reversed, and Beurling sighted carefully and opened fire. Cannon shells at point-blank range ripped a wing off the Macchi and it fell into an uncontrollable spin.

More planes had joined the scrap. As Beurling watched, a section of 109's jumped a formation of five Hurricanes. One of the British planes rolled on its back and plunged to the ground. There was no parachute. A Spitfire vengefully lunged at the victorious 109, its cannon cutting chunks out of the wings and fuselage.

Too far away to help, Beurling turned his attention to the bombers. Ahead of him loomed a JU-88. Its rear gunner spotted the approaching Spit and tracers lanced out at the Canadian. Closing rapidly, Beurling hammered out a long burst, and flame exploded from the bomber. Number two. A glance at the fuel gauge revealed that his tanks were almost empty so the Canadian dived for the water, flattened out, and skimmed up over the cliffs of Malta, heading home. But the fight was not over yet. Unnoticed, he had slipped past three ME-109's that were strafing the airfield. They were closing rapidly on another Spitfire, which was circling the field for a landing, obviously short of fuel. The opportunity was too good to miss. Beurling slipped up on the nearest Messerschmitt and fired. His cannon shells exploded along the fuselage, and the low-flying German plane crashed into a wrecked building. Number three. Another Messerschmitt, intent on strafing, headed right towards Beurling. Again his guns chattered and smoke boiled out of the German fighter's engine. Number four.

More Spitfires appeared and, his gas now down to the danger point, Beurling landed. An hour later, he was airborne again. Thirty Stuka dive bombers escorted by almost one hundred ME-109's were attacking a cargo boat that had just arrived with precious aviation fuel. Another ME 109 went down before Beurling's guns. Then, attacking a Stuka, Beurling's amazing first day total of kills was lev-elled at five when his propeller was damaged by pieces that flew off the German plane, and he was forced to make an emergency landing in a small field.

Between July 6 and 29, Beurling downed fifteen enemy craft. By the end of July only seven of the pilots who had flown into the island from the *Eagle* were left. Of the rest, eight had been killed and the remainder evacuated because of wounds or exhaustion. When interviewed by Canadian writer Leslie Roberts about his outstanding successes on Malta, Beurling replied: "I just thought I was very lucky."

By then he had earned the nickname "Diamond Eyes," because of his unerring accuracy. He became the recognized dean of deflection shooting. Deflection shooting depends on the adjustment of the angle of fire to compensate the speed of a moving target. The pilot must calculate how far ahead of a speeding enemy aircraft he must aim his bullets and his opponent's plane are to meet. The planes were fitted with gyro gunsights, which anticipated the angle of fire and helped a pilot make this calculation. Beurling found the special sights unnecessary. So swift were his calculations, and so keen his eye, that fellow pilots said this young sergeant pilot carried his gunsight in his head.

Beurling liked to hoard his bullets during a fight. When he said: "I lined him up and gave him a squirt," it usually meant another victory, for few of his bullets missed their mark. Beurling's combat reports were models of detail. He not only described the action, but often told exactly where and how many of his cannon shells and bullets had struck home. Once he claimed a probable and stated that five of his cannon shells had gone into the cockpit of the enemy plane. Shortly afterwards, a report came through that an Italian aircraft had crashed during a raid that day. Investigation revealed five cannon holes, just where Beurling had described them.

Beurling had few illusions about the work of a fighter pilot. He often expressed respect for the tough job the her services had in time of war, and to him the bomber crews were the real heroes who did the "dirty and dangerous work." He was thankful for his job as a fighter pilot and revelled in the sense of independence of being the captain of his own aircraft. "Most of us went into fighters because it was the softest place to fight," he said.

As mentioned earlier, Beurling thought a wing man was an encumberance. He preferred to fly alone, although it was now standard procedure for aircraft to fly in pair Malta he could flout the new system of team flying with impunity, not because discipline was more lax, but simply because the lack of men and planes made the wing man concept a fond dream. There simply weren't enough planes to follow the team concept. This situation was just fine for Beurling, who enjoyed the dangerous challenge of pitting his own flying skill and accuracy against superior odds.

Even here, though, where the heat of battle left men exhausted and drained, Beurling's combative personality came to the fore, and his competitive nature got him into trouble. During a lull in the bombing attack, Malta's defence forces decided to put on a show of strength with a parade down the narrow, canyon-like main streets of Valetta. Above the marching men, three Spitfires were to fly below the level of the rooftops as the Air Force entry in the parade. Two veteran wing commanders were chosen to make the flight, which would be a dangerous and tricky display of aerobatics. The planes would be so low that people on the balconies of the tall stone buildings lining the street would be able to look down into the cockpits, and any sudden downdraft would be fatal. Beurling was asked to be third member of the formation.

This was a compliment to his flying ability, since he was one of the youngest members of the squadron and still of non-commissioned rank. His job would be to fly straight and level, while the two senior pilots weaved their planes back and forth across his tail. The stunt was a terrific success, and apparently served to show the Maltese that with pilots like these they could be confident of eventual victory over the German and Italian air forces. But Beurling wasn't satisfied with his target role in the manoeuvre. Later, he showed his superiors what he would have preferred to do by flying down the street, fifty feet off the deck, and upside down. The demonstration only angered the two officers.

Canada was beginning to hear stories about a certain hot pilot-called Screwball around this time. The eyes of the world were focused on the Mediterranean, where big battles were being fought. Bigger ones were in the offing, and news correspondents, looking for colour stories from the battle zone, found that Beurling made good copy. One story that did not make the newspapers in Canada occurred shortly after the parade incident. Beurling was offered a promotion to commissioned rank, which he prompty and flatly refused.

The promotion to the rank of pilot officer had been offered as recognition of Beurling's ability. He had already been awarded the Distinguished Flying Medal, the noncommissioned equivalent of the Distinguished Flying Cross, and a bar had been added to that ribbon shortly after. But Beurling was suspicious of any up-grading. One of his main worries was that it was a step towards the responsibility a flight leader, and an end to his days as a lone wolf. His reluctance to accept responsibility for the lives of others may have been motivated by inner doubt. Beurling's only ambition was to fly and fight; in that role he was sure of himself and his worth. He really did not want a higher rank and the hidden reason for this refusal of promotion was probably personal insight and, despite his bluster, a certain humility. It is not often that a man who has made a success of one job can honestly assess his talents and refuse the attractions of higher position and greater responsibility.

By his refusal of the promotion, Beurling was tacitly admitting that he recognized his limitations. Higher authority decided they knew the man better than he knew himself, however. There was also the embarrassment of explaining to a Canadian press why this brilliant young pilot was still a sergeant when less accomplished men had been promote to officer status. In the daily orders, Beurling's promotion was published. But despite the ruling of his seniors, Beurlin continued to wear his sergeant's stripes and eat in the sergeants' mess. His superiors finally had to tell him that he was an officer whether he liked it or not. Fuming with anger Beurling took off the day after the ultimatum and promptly shot down three German ME-109's. In the end he had to bow to the inevitable and reluctantly donned the uniform of an officer.

Beurling's last operational day on Malta was on October 14, 1942. On that day, for the first time, Beurling indirectly conceded that some of the older hands might be right about this business of team flying. Separated from his squadron mates in a sky full of German planes, Beurling was shot down and wounded. The sirens were wailing in Valetta when Beurling, with three companions, had intercepted raiding force of eighty-plus bombers and fighters. "It was one p.m.," he related, "I was closing in on a 109G, riding the prop with 440 [m.p.h.] on the clock. I had given him a burst and was contemplating another shot when I had a hunch that I should break. I often had these hunches and they saved my life more than once. I was about to break when there was a slapping sound on my Spit and my legs were buffeted all over the cockpit." An enemy fighter had slid into position above and behind Beurling's Spitfire as he was concentrating on the Messerschmitt ahead of him. It was a situation that might never have happened if he had had a wing man to protect his tail or to tell him to break before the enemy fighter got into position.

His machine shuddered under the cannon and machine gun hits. The cockpit filled with oil and, with controls jammed, the plane fell into a left-hand power spin. Centrifugal force pinned Beurling to his seat as he fought to bale out of the careening plane. "I managed to open the door and fall out . . . my chute opened with a slap and then the 109 started target practice."

Hanging helpless at the end of the shroud lines, Beurling watched with almost detached interest as the speeding Messerschmitt closed in for the kill, spraying bullets from its machine guns. "The close ones went zip, those that missed by quite a bit went whoosh." (He was unaware of it at the time, but one bullet hit home, clipping a chunk of flesh from his heel.) Then a Spitfire appeared on the scene and drove the German fighter away.

Beurling was still not safe, though. He hit the water, inflated his rubber dinghy, and waited for rescue or death as German fighters wheeled overhead for another pass. He felt like cheering as he saw a plucky little RAF rescue launch leave the Malta shoreline and rush towards him. "The air rescue launch came out with German bullets spattering all around it and they drove on as though at a regatta."

Beurling was taken to hospital where doctors constructed a new heel for his injured foot. He was also presented with the Distinguished Service Order, for, on that last mission, he had shot down four aircraft, scored two probables, and damaged another. His score now stood at twenty-eight victories and he was the leading Canadian ace of the Second World War.

The newspapers in Canada were now filled with stories about Beurling and the RCAF became interested in acquiring him. Still recovering from his wound, Beurling was bundled aboard a Liberator for a trip to Canada. When the big bomber touched down at Gibraltar for refuelling, it overshot the runway and plunged into the sea. With the professional eye of an airman, Beurling had watched the pilot's approach to the landing field and had anticipated trouble. Just before the crash, he had hobbled close to an escape hatch and, by the time that the plane hit, had already jettisoned the hatch to allow the passengers to escape. Despite the heavy plaster cast on his leg, he managed to swim 158 yards to safety. Among the fifteen passengers who drowned were two Malta pilots, both of whom Beurling had saved on previous occasions in the air.

By November he was in Canada, a hero. He toured the country, making speeches at Victory Bond rallies and defence plants. Nevertheless, despite his hero's welcome Beurling was ill at ease during the tour and became increasingly moody. He was particularly soured when a group of girls at one civic reception presented him with twenty nine red roses, one for each plane he had shot down. (He had downed one more while in England.) Beurling thought the entire episode in bad taste.

During this time news reporters probed his private life colour stories about Canada's most famous airman. They wrote stories comparing Beurling with another famous Canadian ace, Bill Barker. The stories noted that Beurling, like Barker, was largely a self-taught flyer and, again like Barker considered something of a rebel. Both men were teetotalers. Beurling was also a non-smoker on the grounds that smoking would interfere with his flying. Another parallel with Barker's career appeared when Beurling was transferred back to Britain. His marksmanship had been noted by his superiors in the RAF and he was posted to a training command at the end of July, 1943. The assignment was to a special gunnery school at Catfoss. Here some of the leading aces of the Allied air forces had been assembled to evolve new techniques of fighter tactics and gunnery. "You're the best deflection shot we've got, so you're going to teach others how to do it," he was told.

Among his peers Beurling came out of the shell that he had built around himself since losing his close friends on Malta. The Catfoss station school was commanded by the illustrious South African ace, Group Captain "Sailor" Malan, DSO, DFC, who had scored thirty-two victories. Beurling immediately became friendly with the famous American P-38 fighter pilot, Major Richard Bong, who had downed thirty-seven Japanese planes in the Pacific. Together, they spent many hours in the mess, outraging the modesty other members of the school with far-fetched stories about own ability and experiences. Their small mutual admiration society was enlarged with the addition of Pierre Closterman, the famous Free French Tempest pilot, who had shot down twenty-three enemy planes, and another French ace, Jacques Remlinger. The four spent hours talking planes, shooting, and tactics.

Beurling spent much of his time dressed in a rumpled, unadorned battle-dress uniform until his commanding officer, Sailor Malan, ticked him off for his unmilitary appearance. He stayed with the job for four months, then applied for a transfer to the RCAF in the hope that he would be ordered to active duty. His application was approved and he s sworn in at the RCAF head-quarters in London.

Now that the RCAF had Beurling there was the problem what to do with him. His reputation for unorthodoxy had preceded him, and commanders who were trying to instil a team spirit in their flyers had no time and little patience to spare for an eccentric but brilliant loner. The problem was solved when Wing Commander "Johnnie" Johnson, DSO, DFC, commander of 127 Wing of the Tactical Air Force, agreed to take Beurling into his unit. Johnson, a Britisher, was the RAF's highest scoring ace, with thirty eight victories to his credit, a man whose ability Beurling could respect. In due course the transfer was arranged, and Beurling joined Johnson's No. 403 Squadron, the same unit the Canadian had served with after obtaining his wings. Johnson made it a point to meet Beurling on his arrival for a quiet chat and made a valiant attempt to break through Beurling's wall of reserve. Johnson stressed the fact that the style of fighting the squadron encountered over France was radically different from what Beurling had experienced in Malta. The concentration of German fighter bases in France enabled the enemy to put heavy formations in the air and any lone wolf found alone by German fighters was soon a dead wolf. Beurling brightened visibly at the mention the number of Huns encountered in the fighter sweeps and paid scant attention to Johnson's diplomatic warnings. The senior officer then tried a new line of approach in his attempt to reach Beurling. He asked the Canadian to take over the job of squadron gunnery officer, hoping the added responsibility of, trying to teach the other flyers his own uncanny brand of aerial gunnery would help Beurling readjust to the team operations of a tactical squadron. But again the Canadian did not appear to be listening. His only comments were questions about the number of fighter sweeps carried out by the squadron each week, and the number of times these sweeps resulted in a tangle with German planes.

Johnson told him the squadron engaged the enemy about once out of every four sorties over France. This apparently did not satisfy Beurling, used to the daily scrambles of Malta. "The Jerries must be there," he said softly, almost to himself. Then, briskly, he suggested splitting the squadron into two-plane elements to cover a wider area and scouring the enemy-held countryside at a low level for German fighters. Johnson was firm on this: "No. In the first place, we must stick together because the Huns operate in packs of fifty planes. Secondly, the flak is so hot over here that if we flew on the deck we'd lose half the boys in a week."

Beurling started on a new tack. Almost offhandedly, he asked Johnson about the new Mustang fighter, a long-range airplane being used as an escort for the heavy bomber formations attacking Germany. When the Wing Commander said he understood the Mustang could fly to Berlin and back without refuelling, Beurling looked thoughtful: "Can they now?" he said softly, his eyes reflective. Johnson wrote later that he could almost read Beurling's mind. With a long-range fighter like the Mustang, the Canadian could sally forth each day and roam the entire Continent looking for prey. "He'd either get himself killed or would finish up with more Huns than the rest of us put together," Johnson said later, in his book *Wing Leader*. That ended Johnson's attempt to win the moody fighter pilot over to his way of thinking.

Several days later, Johnson met Beurling again. It was at night and the British officer was walking near a small pond close to the airfield. A dark shape seated on a log turned out to be Beurling. Touched by the lonely figure, Johnson invited the Canadian to join him in the mess. "No thanks, Wingco, guess I'll stay out here. I'm figuring out some of the angles between the stars," Beurling replied.

Johnson flew with Beurling on several occasions, but a short time later the British ace was transferred to another unit. It was unfortunate, for Beurling had always shown a preference for dealing with RAF senior officers, and Johnson had displayed a willingness to meet the unruly Canadian half way.

Beurling's squadron was part of the fighter offensive assigned to clear the skies of German interceptors so that the bomber fleets could fly unhindered to their targets. Mosquito intruder patrols at night and fighter sweeps during the day roamed the skies over German-occupied territory, attacking airfields and fighter concentrations. It was harrowing work, and Beurling's unfriendliness earned him a dangerous spot in the formation, his old tail-end Charlie position.

Yet he managed to knock down two enemy planes, bringing his score to thirty-one victories.

His first victory with No. 403 Squadron came on September 24. Two weeks of comparative quiet had ended that morning when the squadron had taken part in several inconclusive dogfights over France. In the early afternoon, the Spitfires were up again, escorting a strong formation of Marauders in an attack on an enemy airfield at Beauvais. The bombers had completed their mission and were just pulling away from the shattered airfield when a cluster of enemy fighters came down out of the sun and a free-for-all scrap developed.

Beurling's section stayed clear of the main fight, but over St. Poix, Beurling watched with detached interest as a section of Spitfires from another Canadian squadron, the "Red Indians," bounced a formation of ten Focke-Wulf 190's. His interest became less detached when he spotted a lone FW circling high over the main fight. Evidently the leader of the German formation was waiting for a cripple to break away from the melee, so that he could claim an easy victim. Suddenly the German spotted a target. He tipped the nose of his plane into a dive only to be met with a hail of fire from Beurling's guns. The Canadian's first burst blew away most of the enemy fighter's port wing and the 190 spun into the ground.

A month later, on October 18, Beurling's eagerness for combat almost cost him his life. The incident also demonstrated that much of Johnson's advice warning against solo forays had been lost on the Canadian.

The wing was patrolling over Lille when Beurling spot a formation of FW 190's far below. Calling up "Bandits" on his radio, Beurling half rolled and dived in pursuit. Since it could have been a trap, the rest of the formation maitained altitude and Beurling's wingmates saw his Spitfire vanish into a thin stratum of cloud far below.

The air speed indicator had crept far beyond the 500 mile-an-hour mark when Beurling tried to pull out of his dive. "G" force slammed him back against his seat and his vision faded as blood drained away from his brain. Fighting the controls of the buffeting Spitfire he managed to croak "I've had it" into his radio before he blacked out.

The Spitfire finally responded to the controls and when Beurling regained consciousness he found himself with less than 1,700 feet of altitude. Alone in unfriendly air, the Canadian headed home, hugging the ground to avoid flak and fighters. The rest of his flight had landed and were dicussing his chances of survival when Beurling touched down at his home base, 20 minutes overdue.

In December, he chalked up another victory. This time he was leading a flight in a two wing formation assigned to protect a raiding force of Flying

Fortresses and Liberators from the American 8th Air Force. The target was Ludwigshaven, but enemy fighter reaction to the raid was swift, and the first intercepts came just north-east of Paris. In his combat report, Beurling described his share the action: "I was flying No. 1 in Yellow Section when I sighted an FW 190 cutting in from behind and below Blue Section. I rolled to starboard and cut into the FW which dived away. I turned to follow and took a long-range three second burst. I closed in to 270-280 yards and fired another three-second burst from the starboard and I fired another burst for luck. It went straight down in flames and I saw the pilot bale out." It was his thirty-first victory.

He did not get a chance to raise that total. His sojourn with the squadron ended in May, 1944, when he was disciplined for flying a Tiger Moth too low over his own airfield. Beurling's defence for his misdemeanour was that he had been forced to fly on the deck because of the heavy overcast. The explanation was accepted and forestalled the disciplinary action that had been started against him. But he had clashed with authority once too often. Beurling's resignation from the Air Force was accepted. He now held the DSO, DFC, and DFM and bar, and was the top-scoring Canadian fighter pilot of the Second World War.

The RCAF had its own urgent reasons for accepting Beurling's resignation. His individualism posed a constant threat to air discipline, for with every success he increased the burden of anxiety for senior officers. Young pilots, watching Beurling's victory total mount, would try and emulate his style, with fatal results. Every victory he scored as a loner tended to place the principle of team fighting, emphasized by squadron commanders, in jeopardy. "If he can do it, so can I," fledgling pilots would think as they dived their aircraft away from the safety of the formation to pursue a lone German fighter, only to learn too late that the enemy plane had several friends lurking in a nearby cloud. Senior officers repeatedly hammered the message home to their flyers: a lone pilot is soon a dead pilot. The youngsters just smiled wisely and thought of Buzz Beurling. Even veterans, in the whirling confusion of the dogfight, sometimes forgot this law of survival.

Beurling returned to Canada, but his attempts to start a new life for himself as a civilian were doomed to failure. For a while he barnstormed around the country as a stunt pilot, using a pre-stressed Tiger Moth. He hunted game in Cape Breton with a bow and arrow and worked as a commercial pilot, as he restlessly tried to find a replacement for the thrills and excitement of combat flying. At one point he tried to sign up as a fighter pilot with the Nationalist Air Force of Chiang Kai-Shek in China, but the Canadian Government, fearful that Beurling's ambitions might cause diplomatic problems, stepped in and refused his application for a visa. Then, in 1948, he enlisted to fight in the war between the Arabs and the Jews in Palestine. He left Canada, hoping that he would soon be back in the cockpit of Spitfire, and his eyes shone as he told his friends of his plans. He was looking forward to meeting and flying with four former Luftwaffe pilots, who had also volunteered the services.

Beurling, who had been welcomed to Canada by bands, dignitaries, and thousands of cheering countrymen when he returned from Malta as a hero, slipped out of the count with only a few friends on hand to say goodbye. On arriving in Rome he boarded the small plane that was to carry some of the volunteer pilots to the Middle East. Flying with Beurling were three of the former Lufwaffe men, and the agreed that Beurling would pilot the craft. None of them could know that the Canadian's famous luck had now run out. Just when the war surplus plane had cleared the runway, it staggered. Beurling knew that his engine had cut out. As a veteran pilot he also knew that it is a cardinal rule of flying not to attempt to return to the airstrip in the event of a power failure on takeoff. The pilot should try to use what little flying speed he has to glide the plane down, for any attempt to turn around results in a fatal loss of altitude. Now Beurling broke that rule. His flight path was carrying him straight towards a row of heavily populated tenements. Rather than risk a dangerous crash among them, he tried to turn the plane back to the airfield. With the loss of forward speed, the plane stalled and plunged like a stone the ground. When rescue crews arrived they found no survivors.

Few were aware of Beurling's sacrifice. Although he had been Canada's leading fighter pilot in the Second World, a man of exceptional talent and dedication, his death was given only brief mention in newspapers across the country. One senior officer of the RCAF, on learning of Beurling's death, remarked sadly: "He could have been another Bishop, a distinguished citizen and leader. But I don't think would have fitted into the peacetime air force, where discipline is even stricter and flying more standardized than he had known in war."

Beurling belonged to a breed that is vanishing because the modern world no longer needs it. He was a soldier of fortune, the last of the lone wolf pilots. His unmatched gifts as fighter pilot leave us only one word to describe him— genius. No other seems adequate.

Epilogue

The Royal Canadian Air Force, founded on traditions established by men like Barker, Bishop, and Fauquier, continues to produce pilots of the highest calibre. In Korea, the main Canadian air commitment was in the form of air transport service, airlifting supplies and troops to and from the zone of battle and bringing back the wounded to Canada and the United States. Canadian air crews carried out this monumental task in a manner which earned for the RCAF the highest praise of the United Nations Command. The few Canadians who flew combat missions in Sabre jet fighters against Communist Migs proved to be among the finest aviators there.

Today, the Canadian air division in Europe, a strike-reconnaissance force equipped with the latest jet aircraft, is considered by senior officers of the North Atlantic Treaty Organization to be one of the finest of NATO'S units. Canadian pilots have consistently won the annual NATO gunnery competitions, proving that the sharp eye and flying skill of Barker and Beurling are a Canadian legacy. It is a legacy born of the vastness of the country. The airplane, like the birch bark canoe of the past, has played a significant role in the exploration of the remote reaches of this land. Though an instrument of war, the airplane has been essential to Canada's peaceful development. Most of the commercial airline routes flown within Canada and from Canada to Europe and Asia were pioneered by RCAF planes of the Air Transport Command. Distant towns and villages of the north are now just a matter of hours from the centres of population and industry. And the unfriendly barrens and tundra over which Canada's aerial pioneers flew served in turn to create that special kind of self-reliance that stood Canadians in good stead in the unfriendly skies of Europe.

Although the old days and the old ways are gone, and many of the men who flew "on a wing and a prayer" are gone too, the traditions they created will always provide a solid foundation upon which Canada's space age airmen may build. In this age of supersonic speeds, the technological miracles of aero-space exploration, and the push-button kept of total war, the "seat of the pants" style of flying and fighting set out in the preceding chapters seems as remote and distant as the charge at Balaclava. But while the "lone wolf" and the "ace pilot" seem to have become things the past, Canada's airmen of today lack none of the attributes of their predecessors. Courage, initiative, and determination have not vanished. Indeed, the flyers who now stand on the threshold of space exploration will have to demonstrate new meanings of the word "courage" as they face the awful loneliness of outer space.

Glossary

Ailerons	lateral control flaps at the rear of the wingtips
Bomber stream tactics	bombers took off from different points on the circumference of a circle whose centre was the target. They converged on the target and fanned out again after bombing. This strategy eliminated concentrations of bombers which would attract enemy fighter attacks.
Brisfit unit	Bristol fighter unit
Dead stick landing	landing without engine power
Flight	five to six aircraft
Flik	nickname derived from the diminutive form of the Austrian word for squadron
Flying circus	German group of about three squadrons
Gong	medal, decoration
Grease-monkey	mechanic
Group	collection of Wings
Jasta	diminutive of Jagdstaffel
Mayday	distress signal from the French "m'aidez"
DH 9 day-bomber	A de Havilland day-bomber. This light semi-fighter aircraft was used for daytime missions. The night bomber was a heavier plane with sometimes as many as four motors.
Panzer division	from the German Panzerkampfwagen meaning an armoured fighting vehicle, hence an armoured division

Rotary engine	engine in which the cylinders are mounted in a circle; both engine and propeller rotate around a stationary crankshaft
Squadron	three Flights
Tiger convoy	convoy of heavily-armed merchantmen; the addition of armament reduced the cargo capacity but the ships could defend themselves. Their greater chance of getting through enemy attacks was calculated to outweigh the decrease in size of the shipments.
Top cover patrol	defensive patrol maintaining the highest possible altitude above a bomber formation or similar group of aircraft.
Torque action	tendency for the craft to spin in the direction of the propeller
Tour	term of duty
Wing	two to three Squadrons
Zoom	a steep climb at full power

Bibliography

Air Aces of the 1914-1918 War, Robertson, Bruce, ed. Letchworth, Eng., Harleyford Pubs., 1959.

Barrett, William Edmund, *The First War's Planes.* Greenwich, Conn., Fawcett Pubs., 1960.

Baumbach, Werner, *The Life and Death of the Luftwaffe.* New York, Coward-McCann, 1960.

Bishop, W. A., *Winged Warfare.* Toronto, McClelland & Stewart, 1918.

Boyle, Andrew, *Trenchard Man of Vision.* London, Collins, 1962. Clare, John, "Eagle for Hire," *Maclean's Magazine.* Toronto, May 15, 1948.

Drew, George, *Canada's Fighting Airmen.* Toronto, McLean, 1930. Ellis, Frank H., *Canada's Flying Heritage.* Toronto, University of Toronto Press, 2nd ed., 1961.

Fighter Pilot, Ulanoff, Stanley, ed. New York, Doubleday, 1962. Galland, Adolf, *The First and the Last.* New York, Holt, 1954. Halliday, H. A., "6 Group," *Roundel.* London, April, 1963. Johnson, J. E., "Johnnie," *Wing Leader.* Toronto, Clarke Irwin, 1956.

Richards, Denis, *The Royal Air Force,* 1939-1945, Vol. I. London, H.M.S.O., 1953.

Roberts, Leslie, *There Shall Be Wings.* Toronto, Clarke Irwin, 1959. *The Times History of the War,* Vol. XVI. London, The Times, 1914-21.

Turner, John Frayn, *VC's of the Air.* Toronto, Clarke Irwin, 1960. Whitehouse, Arch, *The Years of the Sky Kings.* New York, Doubleday, 1962.

Wolff, Leon, *In Flanders Fields.* New York, Viking, 1958.